THE MAN NOBODY KNOWS

Bruce Barton

GA Publishing, Incorporated

Stone Mountain, Georgia

1998

GA Publishing, Inc.
2196 West Park Court
Stone Mountain, GA 30087
1-800-932-5439

Library of Congress
Cataloging-in-Publication Data
Barton, Bruce.
The Man nobody knows.
Reprint. Originally published: Indianapolis:
Bobbs-Merrill, 1925.
1. Jesus Christ—Biography.
2. Christian biography—Palestine.
I. Title.
BT301.B139 1987   232.9'01   [B]   86-31722
ISBN 0-9652894-1-9

Printed in the United States of America

Cover design created by
GA Publishing, Inc., a division of
GA Communications, Inc.

Table of Contents

FOREWORD

The Man Nobody Knows is a self-improvement book. Literally thousands of books have been written in the twentieth century that closely study the lives of great leaders in an effort to help us discover, and to emulate, the qualities that made these leaders successful. Bruce Barton poignantly unveiled the real personality, physical characteristics, and methods of the greatest leader the world has ever known—Jesus Christ.

In a sincere effort to improve ourselves we have all, to varying degrees, earnestly studied the lives of Jefferson, Washington, Lincoln, Churchill, Gandhi, Roosevelt, King, and others—certainly all great leaders. Our objective is to learn their secrets of courageous, effective, persevering, motivating leadership. By closely studying the words and methods of these great leaders, we improve ourselves and our ability to serve and lead others.

Jesus Christ taught us repeatedly by His words and His actions that true leadership is manifest in outgoing, selfless service to others such as our families, our communities, our customers, and our co-workers. This book reveals the key ingredients to success, as well as to true peace and happiness. Remember that the night before Christ knew He was to be humiliated, forsaken, tortured, and crucified His focus was on giving His joy and peace to others.

Christ showed us that leadership is an action not a title. This book inspires us to see Christ's leadership qualities in His compassionate service to others. Without question, to the degree we can apply Christ's methods to our lives, we will greatly improve our God-given abilities to lead and serve. This book will help you see and understand, maybe for the first time, how you can genuinely be like Christ as you quietly go about your daily life.

Approach this book in the same way you would read a book on Lincoln, for instance. Pragmatically study the man, Jesus Christ and his methods from the perspective of your life. Thoughtfully apply His methods to your real life situations and circumstances. You may then find this book to be the best self-improvement book you have ever read.

How It Came
To Be Written

THE LITTLE boy sat bolt upright and still in the rough wooden chair, but his mind was very busy.

This was his weekly hour of revolt.

The kindly lady who could never seem to find her glasses would have been terribly shocked if she had known what was going on inside the little boy's mind.

"You must love Jesus," she said every Sunday, "and God."

The little boy did not say anything. He was afraid to say anything; he was almost afraid that something would happen to him because of the things he thought.

Love God! Who was always picking on people for having a good time and sending little boys to hell because they couldn't do better in a world which He had made so hard! Why didn't God pick on someone His own size?

Love Jesus! The little boy looked up at the picture which

hung on the Sunday-school wall. It showed a pale young man with no muscle and a sad expression. The young man had red whiskers.

Then the little boy looked across to the other wall. There was Daniel, good old Daniel, standing off the lions. The little boy liked Daniel. He liked David, too, with the trusty sling that landed a stone square on the forehead of Goliath. And Moses, with his rod and his big brass snake. They were fighters—those three. He wondered if David could whip the champ. Samson could! That would have been a fight!

But Jesus! Jesus was the "Lamb of God." The little boy did not know what that meant, but it sounded like Mary's little lamb, something for girls—sissified. Jesus was also "meek and lowly," a "man of sorrows and acquainted with grief." He went around for three years telling people not to do things.

Sunday was Jesus' day; it was wrong to feel comfortable or laugh on Sunday.

The little boy was glad when the superintendent rang the bell and announced, "We will now sing the closing hymn." One more bad hour was over. For one more week the little boy had left Jesus behind.

Years went by and the boy grew up.

He began to wonder about Jesus.

He said to himself: "Only strong men inspire greatly and build greatly. Yet Jesus has inspired millions; what he founded changed the world. It is extraordinary."

The more sermons the man heard and the more books he read the more mystified he became.

One day he decided to wipe his mind clean of books and sermons.

He said, "I will read what the men who knew Jesus personally said about Him. I will read about Him as though He were a character in history, new to me, about whom I had never heard anything at all."

The man was amazed.

A physical weakling! Where did they get that idea? Jesus pushed a plane and swung an adz; He was a good carpenter. He slept outdoors and spent His days walking around His favorite lake. His muscles were so strong that when He drove the moneychangers out, nobody dared to oppose Him!

A kill-joy! He was the most popular dinner guest in Jerusalem! The criticism which proper people made was that He spent too much time with publicans and sinners (very good fellows, on the whole, the man thought) and enjoyed society too much. They called Him a "wine bibber and a gluttonous man."

A failure! He picked up twelve humble men and created an organization that won the world.

When the man had finished his reading, he exclaimed, "This is a man nobody knows!

"Someday," said he, "someone will write a book about Jesus. He will describe the same discovery I have made about Him, that many other people are waiting to make."

For, as the man's little-boy notions and prejudices vanished, he saw the day-to-day life of Him who lived the greatest life and was alive and knowable beyond the mists of tradition.

So the man waited for someone to write the book, but no one did. Instead, more books were published that showed the vital Christ as one who was weak and unhappy, passive and resigned.

The man became impatient. One day he said, "I believe I will try to write that book myself."

And he did.

"THE LIFE of Jesus, as we ordinarily read it," the *Boston Herald* wrote, "is what the life of Lincoln would be if we were given nothing of his boyhood and young manhood, very little of his work in the White House and every detail of his assassination...

Jesus liked to dine out. He was the most popular dinner guest in Jerusalem...

The reader is not shocked by this method of Mr. Barton's...Jesus seems even more the being for the ages."

CHAPTER 1

THE LEADER

IT WAS very late in the afternoon.

If you would like to learn the measure of a man, that is the time of day to watch him. We are all half an inch taller in the morning than at night; it is fairly easy to take a large view of things when the mind is rested and the nerves are calm. But the day is a steady drain of small annoyances, and the difference in the size of men becomes hourly more apparent. The little man loses his temper; the big man takes a firmer hold.

It was very late in the afternoon in Galilee.

The dozen men who had walked all day over the dusty roads were hot and tired, and the sight of a village was very cheering as they looked down on it from the top of a little hill. Their leader, deciding that they had gone far enough, sent two members of the party ahead to arrange for accommodations, while He and the others sat down by the roadside to wait.

After a bit the messengers were seen returning, and even at a distance it was apparent that something unpleasant had occurred. Their cheeks were flushed, their voices angry, and as they came nearer they quickened their pace, each wanting to be the first to explode the bad news. Breathlessly they told it—the people in the village had refused to receive them, had given them blunt notice to seek shelter somewhere else.

The indignation of the messengers communicated itself to the others, who at first could hardly believe their ears. This backwoods village refused to entertain their master— it was unthinkable. He was a famous public figure in that part of the world. He had healed sick people and given freely to the poor. In the capital city crowds had followed Him enthusiastically, so that even His disciples had become men of importance, looked up to and talked about. And now to have this country village deny them admittance as its guests—

"Lord, these people are insufferable," one of them cried. "Let us call down fire from Heaven and consume them."

The others joined in with enthusiasm. Fire from Heaven—that was the idea! Make them smart for their boorishness! Show them that they can't affront *us* with impunity! Come, Lord, the fire—

There are times when nothing a man can say is nearly so powerful as saying nothing. A business executive can understand that. To argue brings him down to the level of those with whom he argues; silence convicts them of their folly; they wish they had not spoken so quickly; they wonder what he thinks. The lips of Jesus tightened; His fine features showed the strain of the preceding weeks, and in His eyes there was a foreshadowing of the more bitter weeks to come. He needed that night's rest, but He said not a word. Quietly He gathered up His garments and started on, His outraged companions following. It is easy to imagine His keen disappointment. He had been working with them for three years...would they never catch a true vision of what He was about! He had so little time, and they were constantly wasting His time...He had come to save mankind, and they wanted Him to gratify His personal resentment by burning up a village!

Down the hot road they trailed after Him, awed by His silence, vaguely conscious that they had failed again to measure up. "And they went to another village," says the narrative—nothing more. No debate; no bitterness; no futile conversation. In the mind of Jesus the thing was too small for comment. In a world where so much must be done, and done quickly, memory could not afford to be burdened with a petty slight.

"And they went to another village."

Eighteen hundred years later an important man left the White House in Washington for the War Office, with a letter from the President to the Secretary of War. In a very few minutes he was back in the White House again, bursting with indignation.

The President looked up in mild surprise. "Did you give the message to Stanton?" he asked.

The other man nodded, too angry for words.

"What did he do?"

"He tore it up," exclaimed the outraged citizen, "and what's more, sir, he said you are a fool."

The President rose slowly from the desk, stretching his long frame to its full height, and regarding the wrath of the other with a quizzical glance.

"Did Stanton call me that?" he asked.

"He did, sir, and repeated it."

"Well," said the President with a dry laugh, "I reckon it must be true then, because Stanton is generally right."

The angry gentleman waited for the storm to break, but nothing happened. Abraham Lincoln turned quietly to his desk and went on with his work. It was not the first time that he had been rebuffed. In the early months of the war when every messenger brought bad news, and no one in Washington knew at what hour the soldiers of Lee might appear at the outskirts, he had gone to call on General McClellan, taking a member of the Cabinet with him. Official etiquette prescribes that the President shall not visit a citizen, but the times were too tense for etiquette; he wanted first-hand news from the only man who could give it.

The general was out, and for an hour they waited in the deserted parlor. They heard his voice at last in the hall and supposed of course that he would come in at once. But the "Young Napoleon" was too filled with his own importance; without so much as a word of greeting he brushed by, and proceeded on his haughty way upstairs. Ten minutes passed, fifteen, half an hour—they sent a servant to remind him that the President was still waiting. Obviously shocked and embarrassed, the man returned. The general was too tired for a conference, he said; he had undressed and gone to bed!

Not to make a scene before the servants, the Cabinet member restrained himself until they were on the sidewalk. Then he burst forth, demanding that this conceited upstart be removed instantly from command. Lincoln laid a soothing hand on the other's shoulder. "There, there," he said with his deep, sad smile, "I will hold McClellan's horse if only he will bring us victories."

Other leaders in history have had that superiority to personal resentment and small annoyances which is one of the surest signs of greatness, but Jesus infinitely surpasses all. He knew that pettiness brings its own punishment. The law of compensation operates inexorably to reward and afflict us by and through ourselves. The man who is mean is mean only to himself. The village that had refused to admit Him required no fire; it was already dealt with. No miracles were performed in that village. No sick were healed; no hungry were fed; no poor received the message of encouragement and inspiration—that was the penalty for its boorishness. As for Him, He forgot the incident immediately. He had work to do.

For some, formal theology has diminished the thrill to be found in His life by assuming that He knew everything from the beginning—that His three years of public work were a kind of dress rehearsal, with no real problems or crises. What interest would there be in such a life? What inspiration? You who read these pages have your own creed concerning Him; I have mine. Let us forget all creed for the time being, and take the story just as the simple narratives give it—a poor boy, growing up in a peasant family, working in a carpenter shop; gradually feeling His powers expanding, beginning to have an influence over His neighbors, recruiting a few followers, suffering disappointments, reverses and finally death. Yet building so solidly and well that death was only the beginning of His influence! Stripped of all dogma, this is the grandest achievement story of all! In the pages of this book let us treat it as such. If, in so doing, we are criticized for overemphasizing the human side of His character, we shall have the satisfaction of knowing that our overemphasis tends a little to offset the very great overemphasis which has been exerted on the other side. Books and books and books have been written about Him as the Son of God; surely we have a reverent right to remember that His favorite title for Himself was the Son of Man.

Nazareth, where He grew up, was a little town in an outlying province. In the fashionable circles of Jerusalem it was quite the thing to make fun of Nazareth—its crudities of custom and speech, its simplicity of manner. "Can any good thing come out of Nazareth?" they asked derisively when the report spread that a new prophet had arisen in that country town. The question was regarded as a complete rebuttal of His pretensions.

The Galileans were quite conscious of the city folks' contempt, but they bore it lightly. Life was a cheerful and easy-going affair with them. The sun shone almost every day; the land was fruitful; making a living was nothing much to worry about. There was plenty of time to visit. Families went on picnics in Nazareth as elsewhere in the world; young people walked together in the moonlight and fell in love in the spring. Boys laughed boisterously at their games and got into trouble with their pranks. And Jesus, the boy who worked in the carpenter shop, must have been a leader among them.

Later on we shall refer again to those boyhood experiences, noting how they contributed to the vigorous physique which carried Him triumphantly through His work. We are quite unmindful of chronology in writing this book. We are not bound by the familiar outline which begins with the song of the angels at Bethlehem and ends with the weeping of the women at the cross. We shall thread our way back and forth through the rich variety of His life, picking up this incident and that bit of conversation, this dramatic contact and that audacious decision. We shall bring them together to illustrate our purpose as well as we can. For that purpose is not to write a biography but to paint a portrait. So in this first chapter we pass quickly over thirty years of His life, noting only that somehow, somewhere, there occurred in those years the eternal miracle—the awakening of the inner consciousness of power.

The eternal miracle! In New York one day a luncheon was tendered by a gathering of distinguished gentlemen. There were perhaps two hundred at the tables. The food was good and the speeches were impressive. But what stirred one's imagination was a study of the men at the speakers' table. There they were—some of the most influential citizens of the present-day world; and *who* were they? At one end an international financier—the son of a poor country parson. Beside him a great newspaper proprietor—he came from a tiny town in Maine and landed in New York with less than a hundred dollars. A little farther along the president of a world-wide press association—a copy boy in a country newspaper office. And, in the center, a boy who grew up in the poverty of an obscure village and became a commanding statesman.

When and how and where did the eternal miracle occur in the lives of those men? At what hour, in the morning, in the afternoon, in the long quiet evenings, did the audacious thought enter the mind of each of them that he was larger than the limits of a country town, that his life might be bigger than his father's? When did the thought come to

Jesus? Was it one morning when He stood at the carpenter's bench, the sun streaming in across the hills? Was it late in the night, after the family had retired, and He had slipped out to walk and wonder under the stars? Nobody knows. All we can be sure of is this—that the consciousness of His divinity must have come to Him in a time of solitude, of awe in the presence of Nature. The Western Hemisphere has been fertile in material progress, but the great religions have all come out of the East. The deserts are a symbol of the infinite; the vast spaces that divide men from the stars fill the human soul with wonder. Somewhere, at some unforgettable hour, the daring filled His heart. He knew that He was bigger than Nazareth.

Another young man had grown up near by and was beginning to be heard from in the larger world. His name was John. How much the two boys may have seen of each other we do not know; but certainly the younger, Jesus, looked up to and admired His handsome, fearless cousin. We can imagine with what eager interest He must have listened to the reports of John's impressive reception at the capital. He was the sensation of that season. The fashionable folk of the city were flocking out to the river to hear his denunciations; some of them even accepted his demand for repentance and were baptized. His fame grew; his uncompromising speeches were quoted far and wide. The businessmen of Nazareth who had been up to Jerusalem brought back stories and quotations. There was considerable head wagging as there always is; these folk had known of John as a boy; they could hardly believe that he was as much of a man as the world seemed to think. But there was one who had no doubts. A day came when He was missing from the carpenter shop; the sensational news spread through the streets that He had gone to Jerusalem, to John, to be baptized.

John's reception of Him was flattering. During the ceremony of baptism and for the rest of that day Jesus was in a state of splendid exultation. No shadow of a doubt darkened His enthusiasm. He was going to do the big things which John had done; He felt the power stirring in Him; He was all eager to begin. Then the day closed and the night descended, and with it came the doubts. The narrative describes them as a threefold temptation and introduces Satan to add to the dramatic quality of the event. In our simple story we need not spend much time with the description of Satan. We do not know whether he is to be regarded as a personality or as a personification of an inner experience. The temptation is more real without him, more akin to our own trials and doubts. With him or without him, however, the meaning of the experience is clear.

This is its meaning: the day of supreme assurance had passed; the days of fearful misgiving had come. What man of outstanding genius has ever been allowed to escape them? For how many days and weeks do you think the soul of Lincoln must have been tortured? Inside himself he felt his power, but where and when would opportunity come? Must he forever ride the country circuit, and sit in a dingy office settling a community's petty disputes? Had he perhaps mistaken the inner message? Was he, after all, only a common fellow—a fair country lawyer and a good teller of jokes? Those who rode with him on the circuit testify to his terrifying moods of silence. What solemn thoughts besieged him in those silences? What fear of failure? What futile rebellion at the narrow limits of his life?

The days of Jesus' doubt are set down as forty in number. It is easy to imagine that lonely struggle. He had left a good trade among people who knew and trusted Him— and for what? To become a wandering preacher, talking to folks who never heard of Him? And what was He to talk about? How, with His lack of experience, should He find words for His message? Where should He begin? Who would listen? *Would* they listen? Hadn't He perhaps made a mistake? Satan, says the narrative, tempted Him, saying: "You are hungry; here are stones. Make them into bread." The temptation of material success. It was entirely unnecessary for Him to be hungry *ever*. He had a good trade; He knew well enough that His organizing ability was better than Joseph's. He could build up a far more prosperous business and acquire comfort and wealth. Why not?

Satan comes in again, according to the narrative, taking Him up into a high mountain and showing Him the kingdoms of the world. "All these can be yours, if you will only compromise." He could go to Jerusalem and enter the priesthood; that was a sure road to distinction. He could do good in that way, and have the satisfaction of success as well. Or He might enter the public service and seek political leadership. There was plenty of discontent on which He could have capitalized, and He knew the farmer and the laborer. He was one of them; they would listen to Him.

For forty days and nights the incessant fight went on, but, once settled, it was settled forever. In the calm of that wilderness there came the majestic conviction which is the very soul of leadership—the faith that His spirit was linked with the Eternal, that God had sent Him into the world to do a work which no one else could do, which—if He neglected it—would never be done. Magnify this temptation scene as greatly as you will; say that God spoke more clearly to Him than to anyone else who has ever lived. It is true. But to *every* man of vision the clear Voice speaks; there is no great leadership where there is not a mystic. Nothing splendid has ever been achieved except by those who dared believe that something inside themselves was superior to circumstance. To choose the sure thing is treason to the soul...

If this was not the meaning of the forty days in the wilderness, if Jesus did not have a *real* temptation which might have ended in His going back to the bench at Nazareth, then the forty days' struggle has no real significance to us. The youth who had been a carpenter stayed in the wilderness; a man came out. Not the full-fledged Master who within the shadow of the cross could cry,

"I have overcome the world." He had still much growth to make, much progress in vision and self-confidence. But the beginnings were there. Men who looked on Him from that hour felt the authority of one who has put his spiritual house in order and knows clearly what he is about.

The mastery of ideas, the achievement of ideals—what we call success is always exciting; we never grow tired of asking what and how. What, then, were the principal elements in His power over men? How was it that the boy from a country village became the greatest leader?

First of all, He must have had the voice and manner of the leader—the personal magnetism which begets loyalty and commands respect. The beginnings of it were present in Him even as a boy. John felt them. On the day when John looked up from the river where he was baptizing converts and saw Jesus standing on the bank, he drew back in protest. "I have need to be baptized of thee," he exclaimed, "and comest thou to me?" The lesser man recognized the greater instinctively. We speak of personal magnetism as though there were something mysterious about it—a magic quality bestowed on one in a thousand and denied to all the rest. This is not true. The essential element in personal magnetism is a consuming sincerity—an overwhelming faith in the importance of the work one has to do. Emerson said, "What you *are* thunders so loud I can't hear what you say." The hardened French captain, Robert de Baudricourt, could hardly be expected to believe a peasant girl's story about heavenly voices promising she would do what the Dauphin's armies couldn't. Yet he gave Joan of Arc her first sword.

Most of us go through the world mentally divided against ourselves. We wonder whether we are in the right jobs, whether we are making the right investments, whether, after all, anything is as important as it seems to be. Our enemies are those of our own being and creation. Instinctively we wait for a commanding voice, for one who shall say authoritatively, "I have the truth. This way lies happiness and salvation." There was in Jesus supremely that quality of conviction.

Even very prominent people were moved by it. Jesus had been in Jerusalem only a day or two when there came a knock at His door at night. He opened it to find Nicodemus, one of the principal men of the city, a member of the Sanhedrin, a supreme court judge. One feels the dramatic quality of the meeting—the young, almost unknown teacher and the great man, half curious, half convinced. It would have been easy to make a mistake. Jesus might very naturally have expressed His sense of honor at the visit, might have said: "I appreciate your coming, sir. You are an older man and successful. I am just starting on my work. I should like to have you advise me as to how I may best proceed." But there was no such note in the interview—no effort to make it easy for this notable visitor to become a convert. One catches his breath involuntarily at the audacity of the speech:

"Verily, verily, I say to you, Nicodemus, except you are

born again you can not see the kingdom of Heaven." And a few moments later, "If I have told you earthly things and you have not believed, how shall you believe if I tell you heavenly things?"

The famous visitor did not enroll as a disciple, was not invited to enroll; but he never forgot the impression made by the young man's amazing self-assurance. In a few weeks the crowds along the shores of the Sea of Galilee were to feel the same power and respond to it. They were quite accustomed to the discourses of the Scribes and Pharisees—long, involved arguments backed up by many citations from the law. But this teacher was different. He quoted nobody; His own word was offered as sufficient. He taught as "one having authority and not as the scribes."

Still later we have yet more striking proof of the power that supreme conviction can carry. At this date He had become so large a public influence as to threaten the peace of the rulers, and they sent a detachment of soldiers to arrest Him. They were stern men, presumably immune to sentiment. They returned, after a while, empty-handed.

"What's the matter?" their commander demanded angrily. "Why didn't you bring Him in?"

And they, smarting under their failure and hardly knowing how to explain it, could make only a surly excuse.

"You'll have to send someone else," they said. "We don't want to go against Him. *Never man so spake.*"

They were armed; He had no defense but His manner and tone, but these were enough. In any crowd and in any circumstances the leader stands out. By the power of his faith in himself he commands, and men instinctively obey.

This blazing conviction was the first and greatest element in the success of Jesus. The second was His powerful gift of picking men and recognizing hidden capacities in them. It must have amazed Nicodemus when he learned the names of the twelve whom the young teacher had chosen to be His associates. What a list! Not a single well-known person on it. Nobody who had ever accomplished anything. A haphazard collection of fishermen and small-town businessmen, and one tax collector—a member of the most hated element in the community. What a crowd!

Nowhere is there such a startling example of success in leadership as the way in which that organization was brought together. Take the tax collector, Matthew, as the most striking instance. His occupation carried a heavy weight of social ostracism, but it was profitable. He was probably well-to-do according to the simple standards of the neighborhood; certainly he was a busy man and not subject to impulsive action. His addition to the group of disciples is told in a single sentence:

"And *as Jesus passed by*, he called Matthew."

Amazing. No argument; no pleading. A small leader would have been compelled to set up the advantages of the opportunity. "Of course you are doing well where you are and making money," He might have said. "I can't offer you as much as you are getting; in fact you may have some difficulty making ends meet. But I think we are going to have an interesting time and shall probably accomplish a big work." Such a conversation would have been met with Matthew's reply that he would "have to think it over," and the world would never have heard his name.

There was no such trifling with Jesus. *As He passed by* He called Matthew. No leader in the world can read that sentence without acknowledging that here indeed is the Master.

He had the born leader's gift for seeing powers in men of which they themselves were often almost unconscious. One day as He was coming into a certain town a tremendous crowd pressed around Him. There was a rich man named Zacchaeus in the town, small in stature, but with such keen business ability that he had got himself generally disliked. Being curious to see the distinguished visitor, he had climbed up into a tree. Imagine his surprise when Jesus stopped under the tree and commanded him to come down, saying, "Today I intend to eat at your house." The crowd was stunned. Some of the bolder spirits took it on themselves to tell Jesus of His social blunder. He couldn't afford to make the mistake of visiting Zacchaeus, they said. Their protests were without avail. They saw in Zacchaeus merely a dishonest and greedy little man; He saw in him a person of unusual generosity and a fine sense of justice, who needed only to have those qualities revealed by someone who understood. So with Matthew—the crowd saw only a despised taxgatherer. Jesus saw the potential writer of a book which will live forever.

So also with that "certain Centurion," who is one of the anonymous characters in history that every businessman would like to meet. The disciples brought him to Jesus with some misgivings and apology. They said, "Of course this man is a Roman employee, and you may reprove us for introducing him. But really he is a very good fellow, a generous man and a respecter of our faith." Jesus and the Centurion looking at each other found an immediate bond of union—each responding to the other's strength.

Said the Centurion: "Master, my servant is ill; but it is unnecessary for you to visit my house. I understand how such things are done, for I, too, am a man of authority; I say to this man 'Go' and he goeth; and to another 'Come,' and he cometh; and to my servant, 'Do this,' and he doeth it. Therefore, speak the word only, and I know my servant will be healed."

Jesus' face kindled with admiration. "I have not found anywhere such faith as this," He exclaimed. This man understood Him. The Centurion knew from his own experience that authority depends on faith, and that faith may depend on authority. Every businessman, every leader in any field today, knows—or should know—what the Centurion knew.

Having gathered together His organization, there remained for Jesus the tremendous task of training it. And herein lay the third great element of His success—His vast unending patience. The Church has attached to each of the disciples the title of Saint, and it may be that thinking of them exclusively as Saints robs us of an essential reality. They were very far from sainthood when He picked them up. For three years He had them with Him day and night, His whole energy and resources poured out in an effort to create an understanding in them. Yet through it all they never fully understood. We have seen, at the beginning of this chapter, an example of their petulance. The narratives are full of similar discouragements.

In spite of all He could do or say, they were persuaded that He planned to overthrow the Roman power and set Himself up as ruler in Jerusalem. Hence they never tired of wrangling as to how the offices should be divided. Two of them, James and John, got their mother to come to Him and ask that her sons might sit, one on His right hand and one on His left. When the other ten heard of it, they were angry with James and John; but Jesus never lost His patience. He believed that the way to get faith out of men is to show that you have faith in them.

Of all the disciples Simon was most noisy and aggressive. It was he who was always volunteering advice, forever proclaiming the stanchness of his own courage and faith. One day Jesus said to him, "Before the cock crows tomorrow you will deny me thrice." Simon was indignant. Though they killed him, he cried, he would never deny! Jesus merely smiled—and that night it happened...A lesser leader would have dropped Simon. "You have had your chance," he would have said, "I am sorry, but I must have men around me on whom I can depend." Jesus had the rare understanding that the same man will usually not make the same mistake twice. To this frail, very human, very likable former fisherman He spoke no work of rebuke. Instead He kept His faith that Peter would carry on bravely. It was daring, but He knew His man. The shame of the denial had tempered the iron of that nature like fire; from that time on there was no faltering in Peter even at the death.

The Bible presents an interesting collection of contrasts in this matter of executive ability. Samson had almost all the attributes of leadership. He was physically powerful and handsome; he had the great courage to which men always respond. No man was ever given a finer opportunity to free his countrymen from the oppressors and build up a great place of power for himself. Yet Samson failed miserably. He could do wonders singlehanded, but could not organize.

Moses started out under same handicap. He tried to be everything and do everything—and was almost on the verge of failure. It was his father-in-law, Jethro, who saved him from calamity. Said that shrewd old man: "The thing that thou doest is not good. Thou wilt surely wear away, both thou and this people that is with thee, for this thing is too heavy for thee, for thou art not able to perform it thyself alone."

Moses took the advice and associated with himself a

partner, Aaron, who was strong where he was weak. They supplemented each other and together achieved what neither of them could have done alone.

John the Baptist had the same lack. He could denounce, but he could not construct. He drew crowds who were willing to repent at his command, but he had no program for them after their repentance. They waited for him to organize them for some sort of effective service, but he was no organizer. So his followers drifted away and his movement gradually collapsed. The same thing might have happened to the work of Jesus. He started with much less than John and a much smaller group of followers. He had only twelve, and they were untrained, simple men, with elementary weakness and passions. Yet because of the fire of His personal conviction, because of His marvelous instinct for discovering their latent powers, and because of His unwavering faith and patience, He molded them into an organization which carried on victoriously. Within a very few years after His death, it was reported in a far-off corner of the Roman Empire that "these who have turned the world upside down have come hither also." A few decades later the proud Emperor himself bowed his head to the teachings of this Nazareth carpenter, transmitted through common men.

CHAPTER 2

THE OUTDOOR MAN

TO MOST of the crowd there was nothing unusual in the scene. That is the tragedy of it.

The air was filthy with the smell of animals and human beings herded together. Men and women trampled one another, crying aloud their imprecations. At one side of the court were the pens of the cattle; the dove cages at the other. In the foreground, hard-faced priests and money-changers sat behind long tables, exacting the utmost farthing from those who came to buy. One would never imagine that this was a place of worship. Yet it was the Temple—the center of the religious life of the nation. And to the crowds who jammed its courts the spectacle seemed perfectly normal.

That was the tragedy of it.

Standing a little apart from the rest, the young man from Nazareth watched in amazement which deepened gradually into anger. It was no familiar sight to Him. He had not been in the Temple since His twelfth year, when Joseph and Mary took Him up to be legally enrolled as a son of the law. His chief memory of that previous visit was of a long conversation with certain old men in a quiet room. He had not witnessed the turmoil in the outer courts, or, if He had, it made small impression on His youthful mind.

But this day was different. For weeks He had looked forward to the visit, planning the journey with a company of Galilean pilgrims who tramped all day and spent the nights in their tents under the open sky. To be sure some of the older ones muttered about the extortions of the money-changers. A woman told how the lamb, which she had raised with so much devotion the previous year, had been scornfully rejected by the priests, who directed her to buy from the dealers. An old man related his experience. He had brought down the savings of months to purchase his gift, and the money-changers converted his provincial currency into the Temple coin at a robber's rate. Other pilgrims had similar stories, but after all they were old people, prone to complain. The journey and the sacrifice were worth the cost. One must expect to pay for so great a privilege.

So the young man may have thought the night before; but today He faced the sordid reality, and His cheeks flushed. A woman's shrill tones pierced His reverie like a knife; He turned to see a peasant mother protesting vainly against a ruthless exaction. An unruly animal threatened to break through the bars, and a part of the crowd fell back with cries of terror. A money-changer with the face of a pig leaned gloatingly over his hoard...The young man had picked up a handful of cords from the pavement and half unconsciously now was braiding them into a whip, watching the whole scene silently.

And suddenly, without a word of warning, He strode to the table where the fat money-changer sat, and hurled it violently across the court. The startled robber lurched forward, grasping at his gains, lost his balance and fell sprawling on the ground. Another step and a second table was overturned, and another and another. The crowd, which had melted back at the start, began to catch a glimmering of what was up and surged forward around the young man. He strode on, looking neither to right nor left. He reached the counters where the dove cages stood; with quick sure movements the cages were opened and the occupants released. Brushing aside the group of dealers who had taken their stand in front of the cattle pens, He threw down the bars and drove the bellowing animals out through the crowd and into the streets, striking vigorous blows with His little whip.

The whole thing happened so quickly that the priests were swept off their feet. Now, however, they collected themselves and bore down on Him in a body. Who was

He that dared this act of defiance? Where had He come from? By what authority did He presume to interrupt their business? The crowds gave way again at the onslaught; they enjoyed the tumult as a crowd always does, and they hated the priests and robbers, but when it came to answering for the consequences, they were perfectly willing to leave it to Him.

And He was willing they should. He stood flushed and panting, the little whip still in His hands. His glance swept scornfully over the faces distorted by anger and greed.

"*This* is my authority," He cried. "It is written, 'My house shall be called a house of prayer for all the nations,' but ye have made it a den of robbers."

Stung by His taunt, His accusers hesitated and in their moment of hesitation were lost. The soldiers turned their backs; it was nothing that they cared about. But the crowd burst forth in a mighty cheer and rushing forward bore Him out of the Temple, the priests and the money-changers scurrying before Him. That night His action was the talk of the town.

"Did you hear what happened in the Temple today?"

"Not a man of them dared stand up to Him."

"Dirty thieves—it was coming to them."

"What's His name?"

"Jesus…Used to be a carpenter up in Nazareth."

It was a very familiar story, much preached upon and pictured. But almost invariably the pictures show Him with a halo around His head, as though *that* was the explanation of His triumph. The truth is so much simpler and more impressive. There was in His eyes a flaming moral purpose, and greed and oppression have always shriveled before such fire. But with the majesty of His glance there was something else which counted powerfully in His favor. As His right arm rose and fell, striking its blows with that little whip, the sleeve dropped back to reveal muscles hard as iron. No one who watched Him in action had any doubt that He was fully capable of taking care of Himself. The evidence is clear that no angry priest or money-changer cared to try conclusions with that arm.

There are those to whom it will seem almost irreverent to suggest that Jesus was physically strong. They think of Him as a voice, a presence, a spirit; they never feel the rich contagion of His laughter, nor remember how heartily He enjoyed good food, nor think of what His years of hard toil must have done to His arms and back and legs. Look for a minute at those first thirty years.

There was no soft bed for His mother on the night He entered the world. He was brought forth in a stable amid animals and the animallike men who tended them. He was wrapped in rough garments and expected, almost from the beginning, to look after Himself. When He was still an infant, the family hurried away into Egypt. On the long trip back some years later, He was judged old enough to walk, for there were younger children; and so, day after day, He trudged beside the little donkey or scurried into

31

the woods by the roadside to find fuel. It was a hard school for babyhood, but it gave Him a hardness that was an enormous asset later on.

Early in His boyhood Jesus, as the eldest son, went into the family carpenter shop. The practice of carpentry was no easy business in those simpler days. Doubtless the man who took a contract for a house assumed responsibilities for digging into the rough hillside for its foundations, for felling trees in the forest and shaping them with an adz. In after years those who listened to the talk of Jesus by the Sea of Galilee and heard Him speak of the "man who built his house upon a rock" had no doubt that He knew what He was talking about. Some of them had seen Him bending His strong clean shoulders to deliver heavy blows; or watched Him trudge away into the woods, His ax over His shoulder, and return at nightfall with a rough-hewn beam.

So He "waxed strong," as the narrative tells us—a phrase which has rather been buried under the too-frequent repetition of the "the meek and lowly" and "the Lamb." As He grew in stature and experience, He developed with His personal skill an unusual capacity for directing the work of other men, so that Joseph allowed Him an increasing responsibility in the management of the shop. And this was fortunate, for the day came when Joseph stood at the bench no longer—having sawed his last board, and planed it smooth—and the management of the business descended on the shoulders of the boy who had learned it so thoroughly at his side.

Is it not high time for a larger reverence to be given to that quiet unassuming Joseph? To Mary, his wife, the church has assigned a place of eternal glory, and no thoughtful man can fail to be thankful for that. It is impossible to estimate how great an influence has been exerted for the betterment of woman's life by the fact that millions of human beings have been taught from infancy to venerate a woman. But with the glorification of Mary, there has been an almost complete neglect of Joseph. The same theology which has painted the son as soft and gentle to the point of weakness has exalted the feminine influence in its worship, and denied any large place to the masculine. This is partly because Mary lived to be known and remembered by the disciples, while nobody remembered Joseph. Was he just an untutored peasant, married to a superior woman and baffled by the genius of a son whom he could never understand? Or was there, underneath his self-effacement, a vigor and faith that molded the boy's plastic years? Was he a happy companion to the youngsters? Did he carry the youngest, laughing and crowing on his shoulders, from the shop? Was he full of jokes at dinner time? Was he ever tired and short-tempered? Did he ever punish? To all these questions the narrative gives no answer. And since this is so—since there is none who can refute us—we have a right to form our own conception of the character of this vastly significant and wholly unknown man, and to be guided by the one momentous fact which we do know. It is this. He *must* have been friendly and patient and fine; he *must* have seemed to his children an almost ideal parent—for when Jesus sought to give mankind a new conception of the character of God, He could find no more exalted term for His meaning than the one word "Father."

Thirty years went by. Jesus had discharged His duty; the younger children were big enough for self-support. The strange stirrings that had gone on inside Him for years, setting Him off more and more from His associates, were crystallized by the reports of John's success. The hour of the great decision arrived; He hung up His tools and walked out of town.

What did He look like that day when He appeared on the bank of the Jordan and applied to John for baptism? What had the thirty years of physical toil given Him in stature and physique? Unfortunately the gospel narratives supply no satisfying answer to these questions, and the only passage in ancient literature which purports to be a contemporary description of Him has been proved a forgery. Nevertheless, it requires only a little reading between the lines to be sure that almost all the painters have misled us. They have shown us a frail man, under-muscled, with a soft face—a woman's face covered by a beard—and a benign but baffled look, as though the problems of living were so grievous that death would be a welcome release.

This is not the Jesus at whose word the disciples left their work to enlist in an unknown cause.

And for proof of that assertion consider only four aspects of His experience: the health that flowed out of Him to create health in others; the appeal of His personality to women—weakness does not appeal to them; His lifetime of outdoor living; and the steellike hardness of His nerves.

First, then, His power of healing.

He was teaching one day in Capernaum, in a house crowded to the doors, when a commotion occurred in the courtyard. A man sick in bed for years had heard reports of His marvelous power and persuaded four friends to carry him to the house. Now at the very entrance their way was blocked. The eager listeners inside would not give way even to a sick man; they refused to sacrifice a single word. Sorrowfully the four friends started to carry the invalid back to his house again.

But the poor fellow's will was strong even if his body was weak. Rising on his elbow he insisted that they take him up the stairway on the outside of the house and lower him through the roof. They protested, but he was inflexible. It was his only chance for health, and he would not give up until everything had been tried. So at length they consented, and in the midst of a sentence the Teacher was interrupted dramatically; the sick man lay helpless at His feet.

Jesus stopped and bent down, taking the limp hand in His firm grasp; His face was lighted with a wonderful smile.

"Son, thy sins are forgiven thee," He said. "Rise, take up thy bed and walk."

The sick man was stupefied. "Walk!" He had never expected to walk again. Didn't this stranger understand that he had been bedridden for years? Was this some sort of cruel jest to make him the laughingstock of the crowd? A bitter protest rushed to his lips; he started to speak and then, halting himself, he looked up—up to the calm assurance of those blue eyes, the supple strength of those muscles, the ruddy skin that testified to the rich red blood beneath—and the healing occurred! It was as though health poured out of that strong body into the weak one like electric current from a dynamo. The invalid felt the blood quicken in his palsied limbs; a faint flush crept into his thin drawn cheeks; almost involuntarily he tried to rise and found to his joy that he could!

"Walk!" Do you suppose for one minute that a weakling, uttering that syllable, would have produced any result? If the Jesus who looked down on that pitiful wreck had been the Jesus of the painters, the sick man would have dropped back with a scornful sneer and motioned his friends to carry him out. But the health of the Teacher was irresistible; it seemed to cry out, "Nothing is impossible if only your will power is strong enough." And the man who so long ago had surrendered to despair, rose and gathered up his bed and went away, healed—like hundreds of others in Galilee—by strength from an overflowing fountain of strength.

One day later, as Jesus walked in a crowd, a woman pushed forward and touched His garment, and by that single touch was cured. The witnesses acclaimed it a miracle and so it was, but we need some definition of that word. He Himself was very reticent about His "miracles." It is perfectly clear that He did not interpret them in the same way that His followers did, nor attach the same importance to them. He was often reluctant to perform them, and frequently insisted that the individual who had been healed should "go and tell no man." And on one celebrated occasion—His visit to His home town, Nazareth—the narrative tells us clearly that the miraculous power failed, and for a very interesting and impressive reason. The people of Nazareth were His boyhood acquaintances and they were skeptical. They had heard with cynical scorn the stories of the wonders He had performed in other towns; they were determined not to be fooled. He might deceive the world, which knew Him only as a teacher, but they knew Him better—He was just Jesus, their old neighbor, the son of the local carpenter. So of that visit the gospel writers set down one of the most tragic sentences in literature. "He could do there no mighty work," they tell us, *"because of their unbelief."* Whatever the explanation of His miraculous power, it is clear that something big was required of the recipient as well as the giver. Without a belief in health on the part of the sick man, no health was forthcoming. And no man could have inspired that belief unless his own health and strength were so perfect as to make even the impossible seem easy.

Men followed Him, and the leaders of men have very often been physically strong. But women worshiped Him. This is significant. The names of women constitute a very large proportion of the list of His close friends. They were women from widely varying stations in life, headed by His mother. Perhaps she never fully appreciated His genius; certainly she was not without her periods of serious doubt, as we shall discover later on. Yet her loyalty to His best interests, as she conceived them, remained true, and she stood tearful but unwavering at the foot of the cross. There were Mary and Martha, two gentle maiden ladies who lived outside Jerusalem and in whose home with Lazarus, their brother, He enjoyed frequent hospitality. There was Joanna, a rich woman, the wife of one of Herod's stewards. These, and many others of the type which we are accustomed to designate as "good" women, followed Him with a devotion which knew no weariness or fear.

The important, and too often forgotten, fact in these relationships is this—that women are *not* drawn by weakness. The sallow-faced, thin-lipped, so-called spiritual type of man may awaken maternal instinct, stirring an emotion which is half regard, half pity. But since the world began, no power has fastened the affection of women upon a man like manliness. Men who have been women's men in the finest sense have been vital figures of history.

The other sort of women came into contact with Him, too—women of less fortunate experience and reputation, whose illusions regarding men were gone, whose eyes saw piercingly and whose lips were well versed in phrases of contempt. As He taught in the Temple, one of them was hurried into His presence by a vulgar crowd of self-righteous Scribes and Pharisees. She had been taken in the act of infidelity, and according to the Mosaic law she could be stoned to death. Shrinking, embarrassed, yet with a look in which defiance and scorn were mingled too, she stood in His presence and listened while their unclean lips played with the story of her shame. What thoughts must have raced through her mind—she who knew men and despised them all and now was brought to judgment before a man! They were all alike, in her philosophy; what would this one do and say?

To her amazement and the discomfiture of her critics, He said nothing. He "stooped down, and with his finger wrote on the ground, as though he heard them not." They craned their necks to see what He wrote and continued to taunt Him with their questions:

"Moses says stone her; what do you say?"

"Come now, if you are a prophet, here's a matter for you to decide."

"We found her in the house of So and So. She is guilty; what's *your* answer?"

All this time He had not once looked at the woman's

face, and He did not look at her now. Slowly He "lifted himself up," faced the evil-minded pack and said quietly:

"He that is without sin among you let him first cast a stone at her."

And again, says the narrative, He stooped down and wrote on the ground.

A painful silence fell on the crowd; He continued writing. Writing what? Some have ventured the conjecture that He traced names of people and places that brought a blush of shame to men in that crowd. That may be so, but it is more impressive to think that He wrote nothing of significance; that He merely busied His finger in the sand, so as not to add to her discomfiture by looking in her eyes. He wrote—and one by one the thick-lipped champions of morality drew their garments around them and slipped away, until the court was empty except for Him and her. Then, and only then, His glance was lifted.

"Woman, where are those thine accusers? Hath no man condemned thee?" He inquired, as if in surprise.

Amazed at the sudden turn of affairs, she could hardly find her voice. "No man, Lord," she murmured.

"Neither do I condemn thee," He answered simply. "Go, and sin no more."

From the moment when the noisy vulgar throng had broken in on Him, He was complete master of the situation. Those were men not easily abashed, but they slunk out of His presence without waiting for His command. And she, who knew men so much more truly than men ever know one another, felt His mastery, responded to His power and spoke to Him reverently as "Lord."

All His days were spent in the open air—this is the third outstanding testimony to His strength. On the Sabbath He was in the synagogue because that was where the people were gathered, but by far the greater part of His teaching was done on the shores of His lake, or in the cool recesses of the hills. He walked constantly from village to village; His face was tanned by the sun and wind. Even at night He slept outdoors when He could—turning His back on the hot walls of the city and slipping away into the healthful freshness of the Mount of Olives. He was an energetic outdoor man. The vigorous activities of His days gave His nerves the strength of steel. As much as any nation ever, Americans understand and respect this kind of man.

He stepped into a sailboat with His disciples late one afternoon and, being very tired, lay down in the stern and was almost immediately asleep. The clouds grew thicker and the surface of the lake, which had been quiet a few minutes before, was broken into sudden waves. The little boat dived and tossed, and still He slept. His disciples had grown up on the shores of that lake; they were fishermen, accustomed to its moods and not easily frightened. But they had never been out in such a storm as this. It grew fiercer; water began to come in over the side and every moment seemed to threaten destruction. At last they could stand the strain no longer; they went to the stern and woke Him.

He rose without the slightest suggestion of hurry or alarm. A quick glance was enough to give Him a full understanding of the situation. He issued a few quiet orders, and presently the menaced boat swung round into the smoother waters of safety. Call it a miracle or not—the fact remains that it is one of the finest examples of self-control in all human history. Napoleon said that he had met few men with courage of the "two o'clock in the morning variety." Many men can be brave in the warmth of the sun and amid the heartening plaudits of the crowd; but to be wakened suddenly out of sound sleep and then to exhibit instant mastery—that is a type of courage which is rare indeed.

Jesus had that courage, and no man ever needed it more. In the last year of His public work the forces of opposition took on a form and coherency whose significance was perfectly clear. If He refused to retreat or to compromise, there could be but one end to His career. He knew they would kill Him, and He knew *how* they would kill Him. More than once in His journeys He had passed the victims of the justice of that day, writhing, tortured beings nailed to crosses and waiting piteously for release. Sometimes they wilted for days before the end. The memory of such sights must have been constantly with Him; at every sunset He was conscious that He had walked just one day nearer His own ordeal.

Yet He never faltered. Calmly, cheerfully, He went forward, cheering the spirits of His disciples, and striking those fiery blows against hypocrisy and oppression which were to be echoed by the hammer blows upon His cross. And when the soldiers came to arrest Him, they found Him ready and still calm.

The week of His trial and crucifixion takes up a large portion of the Gospels. For that week alone we can follow Him almost hour by hour; we know where He ate and slept, what He said and to whom; we can trace the gathering storm of fury which finally bore Him down. And this is the magnificent thing to remember—that through all that long torture of imprisonment, court trials, midnight hearings, scourgings, loss of food and loss of sleep, He never once ceased to be the Master. His accusers were determined. They thronged the courtyard before the palace, clamoring for His blood, yet even they felt a momentary awe when He appeared before them on the balcony.

Even Pilate felt it. The two men offered a strange contrast standing there—the Roman governor whose lips were so soon to speak the sentence of death, and the silent, self-possessed former carpenter—accused and doomed—yet bearing Himself with so much majesty, as though He were somehow beyond the reach of man-made law, and safe from the hurt of its penalties. In the face of the Roman were deep unpleasant lines; his cheeks were fatty with self-indulgence; he had the colorless look of indoor living. The straight young man stood inches above him, bronzed and hard and clean as the air of His loved mountain and lake.

Pilate raised his hand; the tumult died; a stillness descended on the crowd. He turned and faced Jesus, and from his coarse lips there burst a sentence which is a truer portrait than any painter has ever given us. The involuntary testimony of the dissipated cynical Roman in the presence of perfect strength, perfect assurance, perfect calm:

"Behold," he cried, "the man!"

CHAPTER 3

THE SOCIABLE MAN

A WICKED falsehood has come down through the ages.

It reappears every once in a while, usually in works by reputable and well-meaning writers, and usually in some such form as this: The author will, in his reading and research, have come onto the supposed description of Jesus by the Roman Lentulus, who succeeded Pilate as Governor of Jerusalem. Lentulus' description was detailed, and it concluded with the unfortunate statement: "Nobody has ever seen him laugh."

We want to be reverent. But to worship a Lord who never laughed—it is a strain.

The quotation from Lentulus is a forgery, penned by an unknown impostor in a later century; yet how persistently it has lived, and with what tragic thoroughness it has done its work. How many millions of happy-minded folk, when they have thought of Jesus at all, have had a feeling of uneasiness! "Suppose," they have said, "He were to enter the room and find us laughing and enjoying ourselves! When there is so much suffering and sin in the world, is it right to be happy? What would Jesus say?"

With such compunctions cheerful folk have had their brighter moments tinctured. The friendliest man who ever lived has been shut off by a black wall of tradition from those whose friendship He would most enjoy. Theology has reared a graven image and robbed the world of the joy and laughter of the Great Companion.

It is not hard to understand when you remember the character of the early theologians. They lived in sad days; they were men of introspection to whom every simple thing was symbolic of some hidden mystery and life itself was a tangle of philosophic formulas.

Baffled by the death of Jesus, they rejected the splendid truth and fashioned a creed instead. Lambs were put to death in the Temple as a sacrifice for the sins of the worshippers; ergo, Jesus was the Lamb of God. His death had been planned from the beginning of the world. The human race was hopelessly wayward; God knew that it would be, and nothing would turn Him from his vindictive purpose to destroy it but the sacrifice of an innocent Son...Thomas Paine remarked truly that no religion can be really divine which has in it any doctrine that offends the sensibilities of a little child. Is there any reader of this page whose childish sensibilities were not shocked when the traditional explanation of the death of Jesus was first poured into his ears? Would any human father, loving his children, have sentenced all of them to death, and been persuaded to commute the sentence only by the suffering of his best beloved?

Small wonder that the Jesus of such a doctrine was supposed never to have laughed!

The Gospels tell a different story. But the writers were men of simple minds, and naturally gave greatest emphasis to the events which impressed them most. Since death is the most dramatic of all the phenomena of life, the crucifixion and the events immediately preceding it are set forth in complete detail. The denunciation of the Pharisees (as startling to the disciples as the denunciation of the United States Senate by a barefooted philosopher would be to us); the arrest by the soldiers at night; the trial before the Sanhedrin; the hushed moment of the appearance on the balcony of Herod's palace; the long sad struggle out to Calvary, and the hours of agony on the cross—these were the scenes that burned themselves indelibly into their memories, and all the sunny days preceding faded into less importance. The life of Jesus, as we read it, is what the life of Lincoln would be if we were given nothing of his boyhood and young manhood, very little of his work in the White House and every detail of his assassination.

All of the four Gospels contain very full accounts of the weeping which attended the crucifixion—the final miracle; John alone remembered the laughter amid which the first one was performed. It was in the little town of Cana, not far from Nazareth. Jesus and His mother had been invited to a wedding feast. Often such a celebration continued for several days. Everybody was expected to enjoy himself to the utmost as long as the food and drink lasted—and it was a point of pride with the bride's mother that both food and drink should last a long time.

Enthusiasm was at a high pitch on this occasion when a servant entered nervously and whispered a distressing message to the hostess. The wine had given out. Picture if you will the poor woman's chagrin! This was her daughter's wedding—the one social event in the life of the family. For it they had made every sort of sacrifice, cutting a little from their living expenses, going without a new garment, neglecting a needed repair in the house. After it was over they could count the cost and find some way to even up; but until the last guest had gone, no effort should be spared to uphold the family's dignity in the neighborhood. To this end the poor woman had planned it all in her proud sensitive fashion, and now, at the very height of success, the whole structure of her dreams came tumbling down. The wine had given out.

Most of the guests were too busy to note the entrance of the servant or the quick flush that mounted to the hostess's cheek. But one woman's sight and sympathy were keener. The mother of Jesus saw every move in the little tragedy, and with that instinct which is quicker than reason she understood its meaning.

She leaned over to her son and confided the message which her friendly eyes had read: "Son, the wine is gone."

Well, what of it? He was only one of a score of guests, perhaps a hundred. There had been wine enough as it was; the party was noisy and none too restrained. Let them quiet themselves, say good-by to their hostess and get off to bed. They would feel much better for it in the morning...Or, if they persisted in carrying on, let the relatives of the hostess make up the deficiency. He was only a guest from another town. Doubtless the woman's brothers were present, or, if not, then some of her neighbors. They could easily slip out and bring back wine from their own stores before the shortage was commented on...Why should He be worried with what was none of His affair?

Besides, there was a precedent in the matter. Only a few weeks before when He was tortured by hunger in the wilderness, He had refused to use His miraculous power to transform stones into bread. If the recruiting of His own strength was beneath the dignity of a miracle, surely He could hardly be expected to intervene to prolong a party like this..."My friends, we have had a very pleasant evening and I am surely indebted to our hostess for it. I think we have trespassed as far as we should upon her generosity. I suggest that we wish the happy couple a long and prosperous life, and take our way home." Surely this is the solemn fashion in which a teacher ought to talk.

Did any such thoughts cross His mind? If they did, we

have no record of it. He glanced across at the wistful face of the hostess—already tears sparkled under her lids—He remembered that the event was the one social triumph of her self-sacrificing life, and instantly His decision was formed. He sent for six pots and ordered them filled with water. When the contents of the first one was drawn, the ruler of the feast lifted his glass to the bridegroom and the bewildered but happy hostess: "Every man setteth on first the good wine," he cried, "and when men have drunk freely, then that which is worse; but thou hast kept the good wine until now."

The mother of Jesus looked on in wonder. She had never fully understood her son; she did not ask to understand. He had somehow saved the situation; she did not question how. And what was sufficient for her is sufficient for us. The whole problem of His "miracles" is beyond our arguments at this distance. We either accept them or reject them according to the make-up of our minds. But if they are to be accepted at all, then surely this first one ought not to be omitted. It often is omitted from the comments on His life or at least passed over hastily. But to us who think first of His friendliness, it seems gloriously characteristic, setting the pattern for all the three years that were to follow. "I came that ye might have life," He exclaimed, "and have it more abundantly." So, at the very outset, He makes use of His mighty power, not to point a solemn moral, not to relieve a sufferer's pain, but to keep a happy party from breaking up too soon, to save a hostess from embarrassment...See, the ruler of the feast rises to propose a toast...hark to the discordant strains of the neighborhood orchestra. Look, a tall broad-shouldered man towers above the crowd...listen, hear His laugh!

The Jewish prophets were stern-faced men; there are few if any gleams of humor in the Old Testament from beginning to end. It was the business of a prophet to denounce folks for their sins. Go to the Boston Public Library and look at their portraits. You are moved by their moral grandeur but rather glad to get away. They are not the kind of men whom you would choose as companions on a fishing trip.

John the Baptist was the last of this majestic succession of thunderers. He forsook the cities as being wicked beyond any hope, and pitched his camp in a wilderness beside the banks of the Jordan. For clothes he wore the skins of animals; his food was locusts and wild honey. He indulged in long fasts and vigils, from which he emerged with flaming eyes to deliver his uncompromising challenge. "Repent," he cried, stretching out his gaunt arm toward the thoughtless capital, "repent while you still have time. God has given up hope. His patience is exhausted; He is about to wind up the affairs of the world." Many people flocked out to his camp, and his fiery language burned through to consciences that were overgrown with a very thick crust.

Fresh from the carpenter shop came Jesus to stand and listen with the rest. To what degree was He influenced?

Did He, too, believe that the world was almost at an end? Did He see Himself cast in a role like John's, a Voice in the Wilderness, crying destruction? There is some evidence to make us think so. He went away from John's camp and hid Himself in the woods, and there for forty days and nights He fought the thing through. But at the end His mind was made up. His place was among His fellows. For a time His preaching bore a decided resemblance to John's. He, too, talked of the imminence of the Kingdom of Heaven and warned His hearers that time was short. But little by little the note of warning diminished; the appeal to righteousness as a happier, more satisfying way of living increased. God ceased to be the stern, unforgiving judge and became the loving, friendly Father. He Himself was less and less the prophet, more and more the companion. So much so that John—imprisoned and depressed—began to be tortured by doubt. Was this Jesus really the man whom he had hoped would carry on his work? Had he, John, made a mistake? What were these rumors that came to him of Jesus' conduct—His presence at parties, His failure to keep the stipulated fasts, the unconventional habits of His followers? What did such unprophetic conduct mean?

John sent two of his disciples to watch and to ask. And Jesus, knowing how wide was the difference between their attitudes and His, refused to argue or defend. "Go and tell your master what you have seen and heard," He said. "The sick are healed, the blind receive their sight and the poor have the gospel preached to them...It is true that I do not fast, nor forgo the everyday pleasures of life. John did his work and it was fine; but I cannot work in his way. I must be myself...and these results which you have seen...these are my evidence."

He loved to be in the crowd. Apparently He attended all the feasts at Jerusalem not merely as religious festivals but because all the folks were there and He had an all-embracing fondness for folks. We err if we think of Him as a social outsider. To be sure it was the "poor" who "heard him gladly," and most of His close disciples were men and women of the lower classes. But there was a time when He was quite the favorite in Jerusalem. The story of His days is dotted with these phrases: "A certain ruler desired him that he should eat with him."..."They desired him greatly to remain and he abode two days." Even after He had denounced the Pharisees as "hypocrites" and "children of the devil," even when the clouds of disapproval were gathering for the final storm, they still could not resist the charm of His presence, nor the stimulation of His talk. Close up to the end of the story we read that a "certain chief of the Pharisees desired him that he would dine at his house."

No other public figure ever had a more interesting list of friends. It ran from the top of the social ladder to the bottom. Nicodemus, the member of the supreme court, had too big a stake in the social order to dare to be a disciple, but he was friendly all the way through and notably at the end. Some unknown rich man, the owner of an estate on the Mount of Olives, threw it open to Jesus gladly as a place of retirement and rest. When He needed a room for the Last Supper with His friends, He had only to send a messenger ahead and ask for it. The request was enough. A Roman centurion was glad to be counted among His acquaintances; the wife of the steward of Herod, and probably the steward himself, contributed to His comfort. And in the last sad hours, when the hatred of His enemies had completed its work and His body hung lifeless from the cross, it was a rich man named Joseph—a rich man who would have sunk into oblivion like the other rich men of all the ages except for this one great act of friendship—who begged the authorities for His body and, having prepared it for burial, laid it in a private tomb.

Such were His associates among the socially elect. What sort of people made up the rest of His circle? All sorts. Pharisees, fishermen; merchants and tax collectors; cultivated women and outcast women; soldiers, lawyers, beggars, lepers, publicans and sinners. What a spectacle they must have presented trailing after Him through the streets, or covering the side of the green slopes of the mountain where He delivered His one long discourse! How they reveled in the keen thrust of His answers when some smart member of the company tried to trip Him up! What heated arguments carried back and forth; what shrewd retorts, what pointed jokes! He loved it all—

the pressure of the crowd, the clash of wits, the eating and the after-dinner talk. When He was criticized because He enjoyed it so much and because His disciples did not fast and go about with gloomy looks, He gave an answer that throws a wonderful light on His own conception of His mission.

"Do the friends of the bridegroom fast while the bridegroom is still with them?" He demanded. "Not a bit of it; they enjoy every moment of his stay. I am the bridegroom; these are my hours of celebration. Let my friends be happy with me for the little while that we are together. There will be plenty of time for solemn thoughts after I am gone."

This was His own picture of Himself—a bridegroom! The center and soul of a glorious existence; a bringer of news so wonderful that those who received it should be marked by their radiance as by a badge. Of course, He disregarded the narrow Code of the Pharisees.

"You shall walk only so far on the Sabbath," said the Code. He walked as far as He liked.

"These things you may eat and these you shall not," said the Code.

"You're not defiled by what goes into your mouth," He answered, "but by what comes out."

"All prayers must be submitted according to the forms provided," said the Code. "None other are acceptable."

It was blasphemy to Him. His God was no Bureau, no Rule Maker, no Accountant. "God is a spirit," He cried.

"Between the great Spirit and the spirits of men—which are a tiny part of His—no one has the right to intervene with formulas and rules."

He told a story which must have outraged the self-righteous members of His audience. He said that a certain man had two sons. The elder, a perfectly proper and perfectly uninteresting young man, worked hard, saved his money and conducted himself generally as a respectable member of society. But people were gloomier rather than happier when he came around. He never once gave way to a generous impulse.

The younger son was a reckless ne'er-do-well, who took his portion of the estate and went into a far country where he led a wild life and presently was penniless and repentant. In that mood he proceeded to work his way back to his father's house. The father had never ceased to watch and hope; he saw the boy coming a long way down the road, ran to him, threw his arms around his son's dusty shoulders, kissed the boy's forehead and bore him in triumph to the front door.

"Bring a fatted calf," the father cried. "Make a feast; call the neighbors in to celebrate. For this my son which was gone has come back; he was dead to decency and idealism. Now he has cleaned up his thinking and is alive again."

There were high doings in that house that day, and everyone enjoyed them except the older son. He was sullen and self-pitying. "Where do I come in?" he exclaimed. "Here I work and save and have never had a good time. This irresponsible youngster has had nothing but good times and now, when he comes home after having run through his money, they give him a party. It's wrong."

The father did not defend the younger son, but he rebuked the elder. That was what hurt the smugly complacent members of the audience to whom Jesus told the story. The implication was too plain. "There are two ways in which a man may waste his life," the story said in effect. "One is to run away from his responsibilities, causing sorrow to his parents and hurt to his associates, killing his finer nature. That is wrong, and a man must repent of such conduct and change his life if he is to be received again into his Father's house.

"But the other is equally wrong. God is a generous Giver, and selfish getting is sin. God laughs in the sunshine and sings through the throats of birds. They who neither laugh nor sing are out of tune with the Infinite. God has exercised all His ingenuity in making a world a pleasant place. Those who find no pleasure and give none offer Him a constant affront. However precise their conduct, their spirits are an offense...Woe to you, Scribes and Pharisees. You are painfully carefully careful to give exactly one-tenth of your incomes to the Temple, figuring down to fractions of pennies. But you neglect the weightier matters of the law—the supreme obligation to leave the world a little more cheerful because you have passed through."

This was His message—a happy God, wanting His sons and daughters to be happy.

Jesus grew tremendously sure of Himself as His ministry progressed. No passages in all literature are more scathing than His denunciations of the cheerless, self-righteous Pharisees. They smarted under the sting, and the crowds laughed at their discomfiture and cheered the young man who dared to call Himself the greatest of the prophets and who proclaimed that life is a gift to be enjoyed, not a penance to be served. All persons who achieve something have a sublime disregard of criticism. "Never explain; never retract; never apologize; get it done and let them howl," said a great Englishman. Jesus too ignored personal criticism. "No man can expect to accomplish anything if he stands in terror of public opinion," He said in substance. "People will talk against you no matter how you live or what you do. Look at John the Baptist. He came neither eating nor drinking and they said he had a devil. I come both eating and drinking, and what do they call me? A wine bibber and a gluttonous man!"

He must have told it as a joke on Himself and on John, though the Gospels do not say so. Indeed, we must often wonder how much of His humor has been lost to us by the literal-mindedness of His chroniclers. How about that incident, for example, at the pool of Bethesda? The pool was in Jerusalem near the sheep market and was supposed to have magic properties. Hundreds of sick people were left along the edges to wait for the moment when the waters would be stirred by the visit of an angel from Heaven; whoever managed to get into the water first, after the stirring, was healed. Passing by it one afternoon, Jesus heard the whining voice of an old fellow who had been lying there for thirty-eight years. Every time the pool stirred, he made a half-hearted effort to jump in; but there was always someone with more determination or more helpful friends. So the old chap would drop back onto his couch and bemoan his hard luck. He was bemoaning it on this day when Jesus stopped and looked at him with a whimsical smile.

"Wilt thou be made whole?" Jesus demanded.

The old man was instantly resentful. What an absurd question! Of course he wanted to be made whole! Hadn't he been trying for thirty-eight years? Why annoy him with such an impertinence?

The smile on the face of Jesus broadened. He knew better. Enjoying poor health was the old fellow's profession. He was a marked man in those parts; in the daily grumblings when the sufferers aired their complaints he was the principal speaker. Nobody had so many pains as he; no other symptoms were so distressing. Let these newcomers take a back seat. His was the only original hard-luck story. He had been there for thirty-eight years.

The keen eyes of Jesus saw deep into the souls of men. There was a twinkle in them now.

"Get up," He said briskly, "and walk."

The old chap spluttered and grumbled, but there was

no resisting the command of that presence. He rose, discovered to his own amazement that he could stand, rolled up his bed and walked off. A reverent hush fell on the assembled crowd, but before they could find their voices Jesus, too, was gone. The disciples were too deeply impressed for comment; they dropped back a respectful distance and Jesus walked on alone. Suppose they had followed closer? Wouldn't their ears have been startled by something suspiciously like a chuckle? It was a good joke on the old chap. He imagined that he'd had hard luck, but his real hard luck was just beginning...No more of the pleasure of self-pity for him...What would his folks say that night when he came walking in? What a shock to him in the morning when they told him that he'd have to go to work!

The shortest verse in the New Testament is "Jesus wept." That tragic note in His story the Gospel record has carefully preserved. How we wish it might also have told us what occurred on the night after the chronic old grumbler was healed! Did Jesus stop suddenly in the middle of the supper, and set down His cup, while a broad smile spread across His wonderful face? If He did, the disciples were probably puzzled—they were so often puzzled—but surely we have the right to guess, with reverence, what was in His mind as He pictured the home-coming of the cured old man. On that evening surely Jesus must have laughed.

Someone has said that genius is the ability to become a boy again at will. Lincoln had that type of genius. Around his table in Washington sat the members of his Cabinet, silenced by their overwhelming sense of responsibility. It was one of the most momentous meetings in our history. To their amazement, instead of addressing himself directly to the business in hand, Lincoln picked up a volume and began to read aloud a delightful chapter of nonsense from Artemus Ward.

Frequent chuckles interrupted the reading, but they came only from the President. The Secretaries were too shocked for expression! Humor at such an hour—it was well nigh sacrilegious! Heedless of their protesting looks, Lincoln finished the chapter, closed the book and scanned their gloomy faces with a sigh.

"Gentlemen, why don't you laugh?" he exclaimed. "With the fearful strain that is upon me night and day, if I did not laugh I should die; and you need this medicine as much as I."

With that remark he turned to his tall hat which was on the table and drew forth what Secretary Stanton described as a "little white paper."

The "little white paper" was the Emancipation Proclamation.

Stanton could scarcely restrain his impulse to stalk out of the room. No one in his Cabinet really understood Lincoln. He was constantly scandalizing them by his calm disregard of convention and his seemingly prodigal waste of time. The friends and advisers of Jesus were similarly shocked. How could anyone with such important business allow himself to be so casually interrupted! One of the surest marks of greatness, of course, is accessibility and the appearance of having an unstinted allowance of time. The man who appears too busy is not always getting much done. The disciples were extremely busy, Judas most of all. He was the treasurer of the group, harassed because expenses ran high and there was no certainty of tomorrow's income. Jesus brushed away such petty worries with a smile.

"Consider the lilies of the field," He exclaimed; "they toil not, neither do they spin, yet Solomon in all his glory was not arrayed like one of these." That was all very poetic, very nice, but it did not fool Judas. He knew that you cannot get anywhere in the world without money, and it was his job to find the money. The other disciples had similar worries. They wanted to get it clear as to their relative positions in the new Kingdom; they were concerned because outsiders, not properly initiated into the organization, were claiming to be followers of Jesus and doing miracles in His name. They fretted because there was so much work to be done and the days were too short for doing it.

But He towered magnificently above it all. Wherever He went the children flocked. Pomp and circumstances mean nothing to them. They are neither attracted by prominence nor awed in its presence. Their instinct cuts through all outward semblance with a keen swift edge; unfailingly they comprehend who are real and who are not. With a knowledge which is the accumulated wisdom of all the ages they recognize their friends.

So they swarmed around, climbing on His knees, tugging at His garments, smiling up into His eyes, begging to hear more of His stories. It was all highly improper and wasteful in the disciples' eyes. With bustling efficiency they hastened to remind Him that He had important appointments; they tried to push eager mothers back.

But Jesus would have none of it. "Suffer the little children to come unto me!" He commanded. And He added one of those sayings which should make so clear the message of His Gospel: "They are the very essence of the Kingdom of Heaven," He said; "unless you become like them you shall in no wise enter in." Like them...like little children, laughing, joyous, unaffected, trusting implicitly...with time to be kind.

To be sure He was not always in the crowd. He had His long hours of withdrawal when, in communion with His Father, He refilled the deep reservoirs of His strength and love. Toward the end He was more preoccupied. He knew months in advance that if He made another journey to Jerusalem His fate would be sealed; yet He never wavered in His decision to make that journey. Starting out on it, His mind filled with the approaching conflict, His shoulders burdened with the whole world's need, He heard His name called out from the roadside in shrill unfamiliar tones: "Jesus...Jesus, thou son of David, have mercy on me."

It was the voice of a useless blind beggar. At once the disciples were on him, commanding silence. Couldn't he see the Master was deep in thought? Who was he to interrupt?...Keep still, blind man...get back where you belong.

But frantic hope knows no reserve. It was the poor fellow's one possible chance. He cared no more for their rebuke than they for his need. Again the shrill insistent voice: "Jesus, thou son of David, have mercy on me."

Jesus stopped.

"Who called my name!"

"Nobody, Master...only a blind beggar, a worthless fellow...Bartimaeus, nobody at all...we'll tend to him."

"Bring him here."

Trembling with hope, he was guided forward. The deep rich eyes of the Master looked into those sightless eyes. The mind which had been buried in the greatest problem with which a mind ever wrestled gave itself unreservedly to the problem of one forlorn human life. Here was need, and He had time...

A long time ago a sermon was preached in St. John's Church, New York, which dealt very severely with the frailties of poor human nature, and put forth, with unctuous assurance, the promise of eternal punishment for a large proportion of the race. Among the worshippers was a gentleman of unfortunate reputation but keen mind, whose name lingers unforgettably in our history.

As he left the church a lady spoke to him: "What did you think of the sermon, Mr. Burr?" she asked.

"I think," responded Aaron Burr, "that God is better than most people suppose."

That was the message of Jesus—that God is supremely better than anybody had ever dared to believe. Not a petulant Creator, who had lost control of His creation and, in wrath, was determined to destroy it all. Not a stern Judge dispensing impersonal justice. Not a vain King who must be flattered and bribed into concessions of mercy. Not a rigid Accountant, checking up the sins against the penances and striking a cold hard balance. Not any of these...nothing like these; but a great Companion, a wonderful Friend, a kindly indulgent, joy-loving Father...

For three years Jesus walked up and down the shores of His lake and through the streets of towns and cities, trying to make them understand. Then came the end and, almost before His fine firm flesh was cold, the distortion began. He who cared nothing for ceremonies and forms was made the idol of formalism. Men hid themselves in monasteries; they lashed themselves with whips; they tortured their skins with harsh garments and cried out that they were followers of Him—of Him who loved the crowd, who gathered children about Him wherever He went, who celebrated the calling of a new disciple with a feast in which all the neighborhood joined! "Hold your heads high," He had exclaimed; "you are lords of the universe...only a little lower than the angels...children of God." But the hymn writers knew better. They wrote:

"Oh, to be *nothing, nothing*"

and

"For such a *worm* as I."

His last supper with His disciples was an hour of solemn memories. Their minds were heavy with foreboding. He talked earnestly, but the whole purpose of His talk was to lift up their hearts, to make them think nobly of themselves, to fill their spirits with a conquering faith.

"My joy I leave with you," He exclaimed.

"Be of good cheer," He exclaimed.

Joy, cheer—these are the words by which He wished to be remembered. But down through the ages has come the wicked falsehood that He never laughed.

Chapter 4

His Method

Many leaders have dared to lay out ambitious programs, but this is the most daring of all:

Matthew and Mark report in different words that they and nine of their fellows were commanded to preach the Gospel *to the whole creation.*

Consider the sublime audacity of that command. To carry Roman civilization across the then known world had cost millions of lives and billions in treasure. To create any sort of reception for a new idea today involves a vast expense and well-organized machinery of propaganda. Jesus had no funds and no machinery. His organization was a tiny group of uneducated men, one of whom had abandoned the cause as hopeless, deserting to the enemy before the command was given. He had come proclaiming a Kingdom and was to end on a cross; He knew He would not be physically present much longer; yet He dared to talk of His Gospel conquering all creation. What was the source of His faith in that handful of followers? By what methods had He trained them? What had they learned from Him of persuading men?

We speak of the law of "supply and demand," but the definition seems misleading. With anything which is not a basic necessity the supply always precedes the demand. Elias Howe invented the sewing machine, but it nearly rusted away before American women could be persuaded to use it. With their sewing finished so quickly what would they ever do with their spare time? Howe had vision and had made his vision come true, but he could not sell! So his biographer paints a tragic picture—the man who had done more than any other in his generation to lighten the labor of women is forced to attend —in a borrowed suit of clothes!—the funeral of the woman he loved.

Nor are men less stubborn than women in opposition to the new idea. The typewriter had been a demonstrated success for years before businessmen could be persuaded to buy it. How could anyone have letters enough to justify the investment of one hundred dollars in a writing machine? Only when the Remingtons sold the Calligraph Company the right to manufacture machines under the Remington patent, and two groups of salesmen set forth in competition, was the resistance broken down.

Almost every invention has had a similar battle. Said

Robert Fulton of the *Clermont*:

"As I had occasion daily to pass to and from the ship-yard where my boat was in progress, I often loitered near the groups of strangers and heard various inquiries as to the object of this new vehicle. The language was uniformly that of scorn, sneer or ridicule. The loud laugh often rose at my expense; the dry jest; the wise calculations of losses or expenditures; the dull repetition of 'Fulton's Folly.' Never did a single encouraging remark, a bright hope, a warm wish cross my path."

That is the kind of human beings we are—wise in our own conceit, resistant to suggestions. Nineteen and a half centuries ago we were even more impenetrable, and we continued so till the discoveries of science in recent years again and again shot through the hard shell of our complacency...*To the whole creation*...Assuredly there was no demand for a new religion; the world was already over-supplied. And Jesus proposed to send forth eleven men and expected them to substitute a new kind of thinking for all existing religious thought!

In this great act of courage He was the successor, and the surpasser, of all the prophets who had gone before. We spoke a moment ago of the prophets as deficient in humor, but what they lacked in the amenities of life they made up richly in vision. Each one of them brought to the world a revolutionary idea, and we cannot understand truly the significance of the work of Jesus unless we remember that He began where they left off, building on the firm foundations they had laid. Let us glance at them a moment, starting with Moses. What a miracle he wrought in the thinking of his race! The world was full of gods in his day—male gods, female gods, wooden and iron gods—it was a poverty-stricken tribe which could not boast of at least a hundred gods. The human mind had never been able to leap beyond the idea that every natural phenomenon was the expression of a different deity. Along came Moses, one of the majestic intellects of history. His understanding transformed humanity. His great truth can be contained in one short sentence: *There is one God.*

What an overwhelming idea and how magnificent its consequences! Taking his disorganized people who had been slaves in Egypt for generations—their spirits broken by rule and rod—Moses persuaded them that God, this one all-powerful God, was their special friend and protector, fired them with faith in that conviction and transformed them from slaves to men who could know freedom and have the courage to win it.

Moses died and his nation carried on under the momentum which he had given it until there arose Amos, a worthy successor.

"There is one God," Moses had said.

"God is a God of justice," added Amos.

That assertion is such an elementary part of our consciousness that we are almost shocked by the suggestion that it could ever have been new. But if you would have a true measure of the importance of Amos' contribution, remember the gods that were current in his day—the gods of the Greeks, for example. Zeus was chief of them, a philandering old reprobate who visited his wrath upon such mortals as were unlucky enough to interfere in his love affairs and threw his influence to whichever side offered the largest bribes. His wife and sons and daughters were no better; nor was the moral standard of the God of the Israelites very much superior until Amos came. He was a trading God, ready to offer so much victory for so many sacrifices, and insistent on prerogatives. It was the high privilege of Amos to proclaim a God who could not be bought, whose ears were deaf to pleadings if the cause was unfair, who would show no discrimination in judgment between the strong and weak, the rich and poor. It was a stupendous conception, but Amos persuaded men to accept it, and it has remained a part of our spiritual heritage.

Years passed and Hosea spoke. His had not been a happy life. His wife deserted him; heartbroken and vengeful, he was determined to cast her off forever. Yet his love would not let him do it. He went to her, forgave her and took her back. Then in his hours of lonely brooding a great thought came to him! If he, a mere man, could love so unselfishly one who had broken faith with him, must not God be capable of as great, or greater forgiveness toward erring human beings? The thought fired his imagination. He stood up before the nation and with burning zeal proclaimed a God so strong that He could destroy, yet so tender that He would not!

One God.

A just God.

A good God.

These were the three steps in the development of the greatest of all ideas. Hundreds of generations have died since the days of Moses, of Amos and Hosea. The thought of the world on almost every other subject has changed, but the conception of God which these three achieved has dominated the religious thinking of much of the world down to this very hour.

What was there for Jesus to add? Only one thought. But it was so much more splendid than all previous ideas that it altered again and even more surely the current of history. He invited frail bewildered humanity to stand upright and look at God face to face! He called on men to throw away fear, disregard the limitations of their mortality and claim the Lord of Creation as Father. It is the basis of all revolt against injustice and repression, all democracy. For if God is the Father of all men, then *all* are His children and hence the commonest is equally as precious as the king. No wonder the authorities trembled. They were not fools; they recognized the implications of the teaching. Either Jesus' life or their power must go. No wonder succeeding generations of authorities have embroidered His idea and corrupted it, so that the simplest faith in the world has become a complex thing of form and ritual, of enforced observances and "thou shall nots." It was too dangerous a Power to be allowed to wander the world unleashed and uncontrolled.

This then was what Jesus wished to send to all creation through the instrumentality of His eleven men. What were His methods of training? How did He meet prospective believers? How did he deal with objections? By what sort of strategy did He interest and persuade?

He was making the journey back from Jerusalem after His spectacular triumph in cleansing the Temple when He came to Jacob's Well and, being tired, sat down. His disciples had stopped at one of the villages to purchase food, so He was alone. The well furnished the water supply for the neighboring city of the Samaritans, and after a little time a woman came out to it, carrying her pitcher on her shoulder. Between her people, the Samaritans, and His people, the Jews, there was a feud of centuries. To be touched by even the shadow of a Samaritan was defilement, according to the strict Code of the Pharisees; to speak to one was a crime. The woman made no concealment of her resentment at finding Him there. Almost any remark from His lips would have kindled her anger. She would at least have turned away in scorn; she might have summoned her relatives and driven Him away.

A difficult, perhaps dangerous situation. How could He meet it? How give a message to one who was forbidden by everything holy to listen? The incident is very revealing:

there are times when any word is the wrong word, when only silence can prevail. Jesus knew well this precious principle. As the woman drew closer, He made no move to indicate that He was conscious of her approach. His gaze was on the ground. When He spoke, He spoke quietly, musingly, as if to Himself.

"If you knew who I am," He said, "you would not need to come out here for water. I would give you living water."

The woman stopped short, her interest challenged in spite of herself; she set down the pitcher and looked at the stranger. It was a burning hot day; the well was far from the city; she was tired. What did He mean by such a remark? She started to speak, checked herself and burst out impulsively, her curiosity overleaping her caution:

"What are you talking about? Do you mean to say you are greater than our father Jacob who gave us this well? Have you some magic that will save us this long walk in the sun?"

Dramatic, isn't it—a single sentence achieving triumph, arousing interest and creating desire? With sure instinct He followed up His initial advantage. He began to talk to her in terms of her own life, her ambitions, her hopes, knowing so well that each of us is interested first of all and most of all in himself. When the disciples came up a few minutes later, they found the unbelievable—a Samaritan listening with rapt attention to the teaching of a Jew.

He prepared to go but she would not allow it. She ran

back to the city to summon her brothers and relatives. "Come," she cried, "and see a man who told me all things ever I did."

They followed her out to the well—these prejudiced, reluctant men and women who, an hour before, would have thought it incredible that they should ever hold conversation with one of their traditional enemies. Suspiciously at first but with steadily ascending interest, they listened to His talk. It is said that great leaders are born, not made. The saying is true to this degree—that no man can persuade people to do what he wants them to do unless he genuinely likes people and believes that what he wants them to do is to their own advantage. One of the reasons for Jesus' success was an affection for people which so shone in his eyes and rang in His tones that even the commonest man in a crowd felt instinctively that here was a friend...

The afternoon shadows lengthened while He talked. Other citizens, attracted by the gathering, made their way out to the well and swelled the audience. Before the evening meal He prepared to go. They would not hear of it. He must be their guest, meet their neighbors, tell them more, persuade them further!

"They besought him to abide with them; and he abode there two days."

Some years later a tired pilgrim arrived in the modern and perfectly self-satisfied city of Athens. He arrived on foot because he had no money for riding. His shoes were sadly worn and his clothing frayed and covered with dust. One would say that these disadvantages were enough to disqualify him for success in a town so smart and critical, but he had other handicaps more fundamental. He was too short and thickset to be impressive; his eyes had a decided squint; in fact, he was not at all the kind of man who commands respect before a crowd. That he should come to the most sophisticated center of the ancient world and expect to make an impression was extraordinary. The principal business of the clever gentlemen of that city was standing around the market place, there to "hear or to tell some new thing." They were the joke makers and fashion setters of their era. They originated new ideas; they did not buy them from the provinces. And as for investing in a new religion—they had hundreds of religions, some new, some fairly new, some old, but all entirely unused.

A fine appreciative atmosphere for the foreign visitor named Paul! See him trudging along through the suburbs and up toward the center of the town. Poor little chap! Wait until the wise ones catch sight of him; they will certainly have a fine afternoon's sport!

Straight on he marched until he reached Mars Hill, the Broadway and Forty-second Street corner of town. A few of the clever ones gathered about, moved by the same cynical curiosity which would have prompted them to look at a sword swallower or a three-legged calf. The critical moment had come. Paul must say something, and no matter what he said, it would be wrong. Suppose he had begun in the usual way: "Good morning, gentlemen. I have something new in the way of a religion which I'd like to explain, if you'll give me just a minute of your time." A boisterous laugh would have ended his talk. A new religion—what did they care about that?

But Paul knew the psychology of the crowd.

"Men of Athens, I congratulate you on having so many fine religions." Nothing in that to which anyone could take offense. The sophisticated pressed up a little closer; what was the chap driving at, anyhow? "I've traveled about quite a bit and your assortment is larger and better than I have seen anywhere else. For as I passed up your main street I noticed that you not only have altars erected to all the regular gods and goddesses; you even have one dedicated to the UNKNOWN GOD.

"Let me tell you an interesting coincidence, gentlemen. This God whom you worship without knowing His name is the very God whom I represent."

Can you see the crowd? Cynical but curious, eager to turn the whole thing into a joke, yet unwilling to miss a chance to hear the latest. Paul stopped short for a moment, and voices called out demanding that he go on. It appears later in the narrative that after his talk was over "some mocked, and others said, 'We will hear thee again of this matter.'" It was not a complete victory such as his Master had achieved at Jacob's Well; but the audience which confronted Paul was hostile, and his initial success was so cleverly won that this story deserves a place beside the one which we have just related. Together they help us to understand the great mystery—how a religion, originating in a despised province of a petty country, could so quickly carry around the world. It conquered not because there was any *demand* for another religion but because Jesus knew how, and taught His followers how, to catch the attention of the indifferent, and translate a great spiritual conception into terms of practical self-concern.

This aspect of Jesus' universal genius may perhaps be best understood by the psychologist and the business-man. From everyday experience they will understand that—except for the infinitely greater value of His work— Jesus was using a method not unlike those used now as the most modern technique of overcoming unreasoning resistance to a helpful idea, service or product. A wise and good man who was also a splendid salesman explained it like this:

When you want to get aboard a train which is already in motion, you don't run at it from the right angles and try to make the platform in one wild leap. If you do, you're likely to find yourself on the ground. No. You run along beside the car, increasing your pace until you are moving just as rapidly as it is moving and in the same direction. Then you step aboard easily, without danger or jolt.

"The minds of busy men are in motion," he would continue. "They are engaged with something very different from the thought you have to present. You can't jump directly at them and expect to make an effective landing. You must put yourself in the other man's place; try to imagine what he is thinking; let your first remark be sincere and honest but in line with his thoughts; follow it by another such with which you know he will not disagree. Thus, gradually, your two minds reach a point at which small differences are lost in common understanding of a truth. Then with perfect sincerity he will say 'yes' and 'yes' and 'that's right' and 'I've noticed that myself.'"

Jesus taught all this without ever teaching it. Every one of His conversations, every contact between His mind and others, is worthy of the attentive study of any sales manager. Passing along the shores of a lake one day, He saw two of the men whom He wanted as disciples. Their minds were in motion, their hands were busy with their nets; their conversation was about conditions in the fishing trade and the prospects of a good market for the day's catch. To have broken in on such thinking with the offer of employment as preachers of a new religion would have been to confuse them and invite a sure rebuff. What was Jesus' approach?

"Come with me," He said, "and I will make you fishers of men."

Fishers—that was a word they could understand... Fishers of men—that was a new idea...What was He driving at? Fishers of men—it sounded interesting...well, what is it, anyway?

He sat on a hillside overlooking a fertile country. Many

of the crowd who gathered around Him were farmers with their wives and sons and daughters. He wanted their interest and attention; it was important to make them understand, at the very outset, that what He had to say was nothing vague or theoretical but of direct and immediate application to their daily lives.

"A sower went forth to sow," He began, "and when he sowed some seeds fell by the wayside and the fowls came and devoured them up..." Were they interested...*were* they? Every man of them had gone through that experience! The thievish crows—many a good day's work they had spoiled...So this Teacher knew something about the troubles that farmers had to put up with, did He? Fair enough...let's hear what He has to say...

It would be easy to multiply examples, taking each of His parables and pointing out the keen knowledge of human motives on which it is based. The examples already given are enough for this chapter. They show how instantly He won His audiences. With His very first sentence he identified Himself with them; it invariably expressed a thought they readily understood, a truth easy for even the dullest to comprehend. And the first sentence awakened an appetite for more.

Jesus knew very well the value of being able to sense an objection and meet it before it was advanced. He went one night to dine with a prominent Pharisee. His presence in any house attracted strangers who found it easy under the far from rigid conventions of those days to make their way into the room, where they could watch Him and listen. Thus, while the Pharisee's dinner was in progress, a woman generally considered immoral came into the room and, kneeling down by Jesus, began to bathe His feet with precious ointment and wipe them with her hair. Jesus knew what that outburst of unselfishness meant to an overburdened spirit, and He accepted the tribute with gracious dignity, even though its emotional warmth must have been embarrassing. But all the time He was perfectly well aware of the thoughts that were passing through the self-satisfied mind of His host.

"Ah," that cynical gentleman was saying to himself, "if He were a prophet, He would have known that this woman is a sinner and would have refused to let her touch Him."

He might have been tempted to put his thought into words, but he never had a chance.

Quick as a flash Jesus turned on him: "Simon, I have somewhat to say to thee."

"Teacher, say on." It was a half-concealed sneer.

"There was a man who had two debtors," said Jesus. "One owed him five hundred shillings and the other fifty. Neither could pay and he forgave them both. Which of them, do you think, will love him the more?"

Simon sensed a trap and moved cautiously.

"I imagine the one who owed him the greater amount," he said, and wondered what was coming next.

"Right," said Jesus. "Simon, seest thou this woman?"

Simon nodded. He began to wish the conversation had not started.

"When I came into your house, you gave me no water for my feet," Jesus continued with that extraordinary frankness which cut straight to the heart of things. "But she has washed my feet with her tears and dried them with her hair. You gave me no kiss, but she has not ceased to kiss my feet. You poured none of your expensive oil on my head, but she has taken her precious ointment, which she could ill afford, and anointed me."

Simon squirmed in his seat. It was not comfortable to be reminded before a crowd of his delinquencies as a host. He had invited this "interesting" former carpenter because it was quite the fad to invite Him. But the whole atmosphere had been one of condescension—the unspoken intimation was "Here's a good dinner; now go on and amuse us with your ideas." There had been none of the niceties; the rich are so well accustomed to being inconsiderate!

The dining room was silent; every eye was turned to the Teacher; the poor woman still knelt at His feet, embarrassed that her action should have caused so much comment, wondering if the incident was to end in a rebuke. Jesus did not look down at her; He was not yet through with Simon.

"She is like the debtor who owed the five hundred shillings," He said. "Her sins which are many are forgiven, for she loved much. To whom little is forgiven, the same loves little." And then with a glance of infinite tenderness:

"Thy sins are forgiven," He said to her simply. "Thy faith has saved thee; go in peace."

It is easy to imagine that the conversation rather dragged during the remainder of the meal. Even very supercilious and self-assured gentlemen hesitated to expose themselves to the thrusts of a mind which could anticipate criticisms before they were uttered and deal with them so crisply.

On other occasions He won His case with a single question—one of the best weapons in the whole armory of persuasion and all too infrequently employed. How often a blundering advocate allows himself to be dragged into futile argument, when by throwing the burden back onto his opponent's shoulders he could attain an easy mastery. Jesus seldom argued. The record of His questions is a fruitful study for all of us who, in our everyday affairs, must deal with other minds. Let us recall two of those questions.

The Pharisees set a trap for Him. One Sabbath day they hunted up a man with a withered hand and deposited him in the Temple where Jesus would be sure to pass. Then they waited. If Jesus healed him, it would be a breach of the Code, which forbade any activity on the Sabbath. They would have that to recall when the crisis came. Jesus sensed the test and met it without hesitation.

"Stand forth," He said to the poor chap.

The bigoted formalists pushed in close. This was their

moment. They had dug the pit cleverly, and now He was about to fall in. The soft light went out of Jesus' eyes, the muscles of His jaw grew tense, He looked "round on them with anger," as He demanded:

"Is it lawful on the Sabbath day to do good or to do harm? To save a life or to kill?"

He waited for an answer but none came. What could they say? If they replied that the law forbade a good deed, their answer would be repeated all over town. The crowd of common men who followed Him were His friends, not theirs—only too glad to spread a story which would cast discredit on the proud defenders of the law. The Pharisees had sense enough to recognize that fact, at least. They "held their peace" and sullenly slipped away.

On another day it was His own disciples who learned how He could compress a whole philosphy into a well-directed question. They were by no means free from the frailties of ordinary human nature. They fussed about little things—arguing among themselves as to who should have pre-eminence; wondering how their bills were to be met and just where the whole enterprise was coming out.

He brought them up short with a question.

"Which of you by being anxious can add a single day to his life?" He demanded. "And if you can't do this simple thing, why worry about the rest? Consider the ravens; they don't sow or reap; they have no storehouses or barns, and yet God takes care of them. Don't you suppose that you are of more value in His sight than a flock of birds?"

How trivial seemed their concern and controversy after a question like that!

In all the three years of His public work there was not one moment when He failed to be complete master of the situation. He was accessible to anybody—in the market place, in the Temple and on the main streets—fair game for the keen and clever. It became quite a recognized sport to match wits with Him. Pharisees tried it; Scribes tried it; "a certain lawyer" tried it. Always they came off second-best. At length the very chiefs of the priests came one afternoon. Lesser antagonists had gone down; now the leaders themselves would take the matter in hand. They would demolish this presumptuous upstart; by the splendor of their presence and their offices, they would awe Him into line.

"By what authority do you do these things," they demanded briskly, "and who gave you this authority?"

If they expected Him to yield an inch, they received the surprise of their lives. His retort was instantaneous.

"I'll ask you a question," he exclaimed, "and if you answer it, then I'll tell you by what authority I work. Answer me now, what about John; was his work in baptizing inspired by Heaven or by men?"

They caught their breath. Their heads came together; excited and disturbing whispers were exchanged. What shall we say? If we answer that John had come from Heaven, He will say, "Well, why then didn't you believe him?" If we say that he came from men, this crowd of fools will tear us to pieces, because every last one of them believes that John was a prophet. What shall we do? Better tell Him we don't know; better get out of here as quickly as we can...

"We don't know," they muttered.

"All right," said Jesus serenely. "You don't answer my question. Neither will I answer yours."

It was a perfect triumph. Amid the jeers of the delighted crowd the chiefs gathered up their fine robes and went away.

You would think as you read the narratives that the wise ones would have been wise enough to let Him alone. Even a child, having burned its fingers once, knows enough to avoid the fire. But their jealousy and anger drove them back again and again; and every time He was too much for them. In the very last week the "Pharisees and Herodians" gathered together a picked delegation of sharp wits and sent them to Jesus with what looked like an absolutely foolproof bomb. They started in with flattery; after all, he was a simple fellow from the provinces—a few kind words and His head would be turned. Then they would catch Him off guard.

"Teacher, we know that you speak the truth," they said, "and that you don't care anything about the authority or office which a man holds. You treat them all alike, and speak your mind bluntly because you get your thoughts direct from God.

"Now, tell us, is it lawful to give tribute unto Caesar or not?"

Very clever, gentlemen, very clever indeed. If He answers that it isn't lawful, you will have the record of His reply in Herod's hands in an hour and instantly He will be under arrest for propagating rebellion against the Roman power. If He answers that it is lawful, He will lose His popular following—because the people hate the Romans and dodge the taxes at every turn...very, very clever.

He looked at them with frank contempt as if to say, "Do you really think I am quite as simple as all that?"

"Somebody lend me a coin," He exclaimed. An eager listener dug into his purse and produced it. Jesus held it up where all could see.

"Whose picture is here?" He demanded. "Whose name?"

They began to be uneasy. The shrewdest suspected that the path was leading toward the precipice, yet there was no escape. They must answer. "Caesar's," they replied.

"Very good," He said. "Render unto Caesar the things that are Caesar's and unto God the things that are God's."

Another repulse for the best legal talent in the city, another good laugh for the crowd, another story to tell in the taverns, in the Temple court, in the market place...wherever the common folk crowded together. In describing the defeated questioners three of the Gospels say: "they marveled at him" and a little later we read, "and no man after that durst ask him any question."

Every objection had been turned back on the objectors; every trap had been sprung on the fingers of those who had set it. No argument was left for them except the final one which is always a confession of failure. They had brute force on their side. They could not stand against His thinking but they could, and did, nail Him on the cross.

Not in time, however. Not until His work was finished. Not until He had trained and equipped a force which would carry on with double power because of the very fact of His death...Every year in our country there are thousands of conventions—political, charitable, business. Most of them are a waste. They are conducted on the false assumption that overselling and exaggeration are potent forces—that the energies of men respond most powerfully to promises of easy victory and soft rewards. The great leaders of the world have known better.

Gideon, for example. When he called for volunteers to fight the Midianites, thirty-two thousand responded. Gideon looked them over critically. He knew the conflicting motives that had brought them there—some had come from mere love of adventure, some because they were afraid to be taunted with cowardice, some for plunder, some to get away from their wives. He determined to weed them out immediately.

"Whosoever is fearful and afraid, let him go home tonight," he proclaimed.

The next morning twenty-two thousand had vanished. Only ten thousand remained.

Still Gideon was unsatisfied. He hit on a stratagem. Down the hillside and across a little brook he led the whole band. It was a hot morning; the men were thirsty and tired. Gideon, standing on the bank and watching, had a shrewd idea that character would show itself under the strain. Sure enough, of the ten thousand, a vast majority knelt down and pushed their faces into the cool clear water, taking long refreshing draughts. But a few were too much in earnest to loiter. They caught up the water in their hands, dashed it into their faces and hurried across to the other bank, restless to go on!

Only a handful; only three hundred. But Gideon kept them and sent the rest home. Better three hundred who could not be held back from the battle than ten thousand who were halfheartedly ready to go.

With the three hundred he won.

It is a higher type of leadership that calls forth men's greatest energies by the promise of obstacles rather than the picture of rewards. In our time we heard Churchill's "blood, sweat and tears" address to his countrymen, and we saw their response.

Jesus was the great master of this kind of leadership. By it He tempered the soft metal of His disciples' nature into keen hard steel. The final conference by which He prepared them for their work is thrilling in its majestic appeal to courage. Listen to the calm recital of the deprivations and dangers:

Provide neither gold, nor silver, nor brass in your purses,

Nor scrip for your journey, neither two coats, neither shoes, nor yet staves...(Matt. 10:9-10)

Behold, I send you forth as sheep in the midst of wolves...

But beware of men: for they will deliver you up to the councils, and they will scourge you in their synagogues;

And ye shall be brought before governors and kings for my sake...(Matt. 10:16-18)

He that loveth father or mother more than me: and he that loveth son or daughter more than me is not worthy of me.

And he that taketh not his cross, and followeth after me, is not worthy of me.

He that findeth his life shall lose it: and he that loseth his life for my sake shall find it. (Matt. 10:37-39)

Watch the faces and the figures. See the shoulders straighten, the muscles of the lips grow hard. There is power in those faces that will not be withstood—power born of the most transforming appeal which ever fell on human ears. The voice of the speaker was stilled at the cross, but the power carried on. It withstood prisons and scourging; shipwreck and weariness; public condemnation and the loss of personal friends; chains, and the roar of lions and the flames. James was the first to die—Herod Agrippa killed him. His brother John, imprisoned for years on the stony island of Patmos, suffered martyrdom in frightful torture. Andrew died on a cross whose pattern bears his name to this day. Simon Peter insisted that he be crucified head downward, deeming himself unworthy to suffer in the manner of his Lord. Nero stilled the voice of Paul by beheading him; but the spirit of Paul which had proclaimed that "we are in all things more than conquerors," began at that moment to have its larger influence.

Just a few brief years and every member of the original organization was gone, but the "blood of the martyrs was the seed of the church." The Master's training had done its work.

The great Idea prevailed.

CHAPTER 5

HIS WORK AND WORDS

JESUS WAS, as we say, many-sided, and every man sees the side of His nature which appeals most to himself.

The doctor thinks of the great Physician whose touch never failed, who by the genius that remains a mystery to man preceded modern science in a knowledge of the relation of the spirit to health, a knowledge still incomplete. The preacher studies the Sermon on the Mount and marvels that truths so profound should be expressed in words so clear and simple. The politically active man remembers best His courage in opposing the most powerful elements in His community and is awed by His capacity to speak honestly without loss of loyalty. Lawyers have written in praise of His pleading at His trial; and the literary critics of every age have cheerfully acknowledged His mastery as a storyteller.

Each man, it is plain, understands that part of His universal genius which with his own abilities and skills he can most nearly approach. I am not a doctor or lawyer or critic but an advertising man. That means that I am and have been concerned with the ways in which words, design and color may carry conviction to people, with the art-science of bringing others to your point of view. It is perhaps not unnatural that I can think of the brilliant plumage of the bird as color advertising addressed to the emotions of its mate. This is, you may grant, a view not unsupported by observable fact.

It has been remarked that "no astronomer can be an atheist," which is only another way of saying that the scientist knows God because he has seen an order so vast and perfect that the idea of purposeful creation must be part of any thought about it.

My view is less exalted, but my purpose deeply sincere. I propose in this chapter to consider some words and deeds of Jesus which persuaded and still persuade men of the wisdom and justice in His teaching. So I have, I hope, seen Jesus as a man who lived and worked, and not as the symbol conventionally displayed.

Let us begin by asking why He could command public attention and why, in contrast, His churches have not done so well. The answer is twofold. His mission was to teach men. But before even He could teach, He must get men to listen. He was never trite; He had no single method. The Gospels show clearly that no one could predict what He would say or do; His actions and words were always new, arresting, challenging and meaningful to the men among whom He lived.

Take one day as an example. The four Gospel narratives are not chronological. They are personal records written after His death, not diaries in which entries were made every night. Thus we cannot say of most of the incidents: "This happened on such and such a day." The four stories repeat, conflict and overlap. In one place, however—the ninth chapter of Matthew—we have a detailed account of just one day's work. One of the events was the calling of Matthew himself to discipleship; hence we have every reason to suppose that the writer's memory of this particular day must have been more than usually reliable. Let us look at these twenty-four hours.

The activity begins at sunrise. Jesus was an early riser; He knew that the simplest way to live *more* than an average life is to add an hour to the fresh end of the day. At sunrise, therefore, we discover a little boat pushing out from the shore of the lake. It makes its way steadily across and deposits Jesus and His disciples in Capernaum, His favorite city. He proceeds at once to the house of a friend, but not without being discovered. The report spreads instantly that He is in town, and before He can finish breakfast a crowd of townsmen has collected outside the gate—a poor palsied chap among them.

The day's work begins.

Having slept soundly in the open air, Jesus meets the

call quietly. The smile that carried confidence into even the most hopeless heart spreads over His features; He stoops down toward the sufferer.

"Be of good cheer, my son," He says; "your sins are all forgiven."

Sins forgiven! Indeed! The respectable members of the audience draw back with sharp disapproval. "What a blasphemous phrase!" "Who authorized this man to exercise the functions of God? What right has He to decide whose sins shall be forgiven?"

Jesus sensed rather than heard their protest. He never courted controversy; He never dodged it, and much of His fame arose out of the reports of His verbal victories. Men have been elected to office—even such high office as the Presidency—by being so good-natured that they never made enemies. But the leaders who are remembered are those who had plenty of critics and dealt with them vigorously.

"What's the objection?" He exclaimed, turning on the dissenters. "Why do you stand there and criticize? Is it easier to say, 'Thy sins be forgiven thee,' or to say, 'Arise, take up thy bed and walk'? The results are the same."

Bending over the sick man again, He said, "Arise, take up thy bed and go unto thine house."

The man stirred and was amazed to find that his muscles responded. Slowly, doubtingly, he struggled to his feet, and with a great shout of happiness started off, surrounded by his jubilant friends. The critics had received their answer, but they refused to give up. For an hour or more they persisted in angry argument, until the meeting ended in a tumult.

It's hardly necessary to say that Jesus did not heal merely to stir, awe and anger doubters. Yet His honest directness had a startling, far-reaching effect. One of those who had been attracted by the excitement was a tax collector named Matthew. Being a man of business he could not stay through the argument, but slipped away early and was hard at work when Jesus passed by a few minutes before noon.

"Matthew, I want you," said Jesus.

That was all. No argument; no offer of inducements; no promise of rewards. Merely "I want you"; and the prosperous tax collector closed his office, prepared a feast for the brilliant young teacher and forthwith announced himself a disciple. Once again we can be sure Jesus' purpose was single. But we can easily believe also that His instant winning of Matthew shook Capernaum for the second time that day.

A feast provided by Matthew furnished a third sensation. It was not at all the kind of affair which a religious teacher would be expected to approve. Decidedly, it was good-natured and noisy.

No theological test was applied in limiting the invitation. No one stood at the entrance to demand, "What is your belief regarding Jesus?" or, "Have you or have you not been baptized?" The doors were flung wide, and, along with the disciples and the respectable folks, a swarm of publicans and sinners trooped in.

"Outrageous," grumbled the worthy folk. "Surely if this Teacher had any moral standards He never would eat with such rabble."

They were shocked, but He was not. That He had condemned Himself according to their formula worried Him not a whit. His liking for people overran all social boundaries; He just could not seem to remember that some people are nice people, proper people, and some are not.

"Come, come," He exclaimed to the Pharisees, "won't you ever stop nagging at me because I eat with these outsiders? Who needs the doctor most—they that are well or they that are sick?

"And here's another thing to think about," He added. "You lay so much stress on forms and creeds and occasions—do you suppose God cares about all that? What do you think He meant when He said: 'I will have mercy and not sacrifice'? Take that home and puzzle over it."

A fourth event to rouse the town. You may be sure it was carried into hundreds of homes during the next few weeks, and formed the basis for many a long evening's discussion. Jesus had been intent only on His ministry. Though He had not sought attention, the streets rang with His name. Indifference to such a manner was impossible.

As the meal drew to its close there came a dramatic interruption—a ruler of the city made his way slowly to the head of the table and stood silent, bowed by a terrible weight of grief. That morning he had sat at his daughter's bedside, clasping her frail hand in his, watching the flutter of the pulse, trying by the force of his longing to hold that little life back from the precipice. And at last the doctors had told him that it was useless to hope any more. So he had come, this ruler, to the strange young man whose deeds of healing were the sensation of the day.

Was it too late? The ruler had thought so when he entered the door, but as he stood in that splendid presence a new thrilling conviction gripped him:

"Master, my daughter is even now dead," he exclaimed; "but come and lay your hand on her and she will live."

Jesus rose from His seat, drawn by that splendid outburst of faith, and without hesitation or questioning He started for the door. All His life He seemed to feel that there was no limit at all to what He could do if only those who besought Him believed enough. He grasped the ruler's arm and led the way up the street. His disciples and motley crowd walked behind.

They had several blocks to travel, and before their journey was completed another interruption occurred.

A woman who had been sick for twelve years edged through the crowd, eluded the sharp eyes of the disciples and touched the hem of His garment. "For she said within herself, if I may but touch His garment, I shall be whole." What an idea! What a personality His must have been to provoke such ideas! "My daughter is dead, but lay your hands on her and she will live."..."I've been sick for twelve years; the doctors can do nothing, but if I only touch His coat I'll be all right."

The woman won her victory. By that touch, by His smile, by the few words He spoke, her faith rose triumphant over disease. She "was made whole from that hour."

Again He moved forward, the crowd pressing hard. The ruler's residence was now in sight. The paid mourners, hired by the hour, were busy about the doorway; they increased their activities as their employer came in sight—hideous wails and the dull sounding of cymbals, a horrible pretense of grief. Jesus quickened His stride.

"Give place," He called out to them with a commanding gesture. "The maid is not dead but sleepeth."

They laughed Him to scorn. He brushed them aside, strode into the house and took the little girl by the hand. The crowd looked on dumfounded, for at the magic of His touch she opened her eyes and sat up.

Now every citizen must have been thinking of this man. Every citizen had to answer questions about Him. Had these things really happened? A woman sick twelve years and healed! A child whom the doctors had abandoned for dead sits up and smiles! No wonder a thousand tongues were busy that night discussing His name and work. "The fame thereof went abroad into all that land," says the narrative. Nothing could keep it from going abroad. It was irresistible news!

He was known by His service, not by His sermons; this is the noteworthy fact. His preaching seems in the light of such events almost incidental. On only one occasion did He deliver a long discourse, and that was probably interrupted often by questions and debates. He did not come to establish a theology but to lead a good life. Living more healthfully than any of His contemporaries, He spread health wherever He went. Thinking more daringly, more divinely, than anyone before Him, He expressed Himself in words of great beauty. His sermons, if they may be called sermons, were chiefly explanatory of His service. He healed a lame man, gave sight to a blind man, fed the hungry, cheered the poor; and by these works He was known.

The church, which hopes to spread widely the news of good work, often receives little attention. Yet it is much more fruitful in such good works than the uninformed suspect. Most of our colleges were founded under its inspiration; most of our hospitals grew out of, and are supported by, its membership; the ideals that animate all civic enterprises are its ideals; and its members furnish to such movements the most dependable support. More than this, the day-by-day life of any genuine pastor is a constant succession of healings and helpings, as anyone who has been privileged to grow up in a minister's family very well knows. The doorbell or telephone rings at breakfast time; it rings at dinner time; it rings late at night—and every ring means that someone has come to cast his burden on the parsonage. A man comes blinded by his greed or hatred or fear—he opens his heart to the pastor and goes away having received his sight. A parent whose child is dead in selfishness comes leading the child by the hand. And sometimes the preacher is able to touch the withered veins of conscience, and life becomes normal and wholesome again. A man out of work, whose family is hungry, knocks timidly at the parsonage door. And somehow, from the parson's few loaves and fishes, the other family is fed.

These are Jesus' works, done in Jesus' name. If He lived again now, He would be known by His service, not merely by His sermons. One thing is certain: He would not neglect the market place. Few of His sermons were delivered in synagogues. For the most part He was in the crowded places—the Temple court, the city squares, the centers where goods were bought and sold. I emphasized this fact once to a group of preachers.

"You mean that we ought to do street preaching!" one of them exclaimed.

But street preaching is not at all analogous to what Jesus did. The cities in which He worked were both small and leisurely; the market was a gathering place where everybody came at some time—the place of exchange for all merchandise and for ideas. The world is no longer so small. Where will you find such a market place in modern days? A corner of Fifth Avenue? A block on Broadway? Only a tiny fraction of the city's people pass any given point in the downtown district on any given day. A man might stand and preach for years at Fifth Avenue and

Forty-second Street, and only one in a hundred thousand would ever know that he lived.

No. Few ideas gain currency unless they may be presented simultaneously to hundreds of thousands. Magazines, newspapers, radio and television networks are now the street in Capernaum. Here our goods are sold; here voices are raised to win our loyalty to ideas, to causes—to faiths. That the voice of Jesus should be still in our market place is an omission which He could soon find a way to correct. The minds He challenged in Capernaum cannot be so different from ours. We are not stirred because we do not hear. If it came to us so directly as it came to the townsmen of Capernaum, could we refuse to heed His call:

> For what shall it profit a man, if he shall gain
> the whole world, and lose his own soul?
> Or what shall a man give in exchange for
> his soul? (Mark 8:36-37)

Suppose His challenge were in every newspaper and magazine; and with it an invitation to share in the joyous enterprise of His work.

One eminent publisher has a rule that no photograph shall ever be printed in his newspapers unless it contains human beings. You and I are interested most of all in ourselves; next to that we are interested in other people. What do they look like? How old are they? What have they done and said? Jesus recognized this trait of human nature. One of the most revealing of all verses to those who would understand the secret of His power is this: "All these things spake Jesus unto the multitude in parables; and without a parable spake he not unto them." A parable is a story. He told them stories, stories about people, and let the stories carry His message.

He might have adopted very different methods—many teachers and would-be leaders do. He might have dealt in generalities, saying: "When you are going about your business, be as kind as you can. Be thoughtful of the other travelers on the highways of life. Take time to look for those who have fared less fortunately; lend them a helping hand whenever you can."

I say He might have uttered such generalities. But if He had, do you suppose that they would ever have been remembered? Would the disciples have recorded them? Would our age ever have heard His name? He was far wiser in the laws and habits of the human mind. Instead of such commonplace phrases, He painted this striking picture: "A certain man went down from Jerusalem to Jericho and fell among thieves." There's your illustration! If you had lived near Jerusalem or Jericho, if you often had occasion to use that very road, wouldn't you want to know what happened to that unfortunate traveler?

"They stripped off his raiment," the parable continues, "and wounded him, and departed, leaving him half dead." Soon a priest came by and seeing the victim said to himself, "That's a shameful thing. The police ought to do something about these outrages." But he crossed the road carefully and passed by on the other side. A certain respectable Levite also appeared. "His own fault," he sniffed; "ought to be more careful." And he too passed by. Then a third traveler drew near and stopped—and the whole world knows what happened...Generalities would have been soon forgotten. But the story that had its roots in everyday human experience and need lives and will live forever. The parable of the Good Samaritan condenses the philosophy of Christianity into a half dozen unforgettable paragraphs.

Take any one of the parables, no matter which—you will find that it is a perfect example of the way in which a new idea may be presented. Always a picture in the very first sentence; crisp, graphic language and a message so clear that even the least interested cannot escape it. "Ten virgins...went forth to meet the bridegroom."

A striking picture, and the story which follows has not a single wasted word:

> And five of them were wise, and five were foolish.
>
> They that were foolish took their lamps, and took no oil with them:
>
> But the wise took oil in their vessels with their lamps.
>
> While the bridegroom tarried, they all

slumbered and slept.

And at midnight there was a cry made, Behold, the bridegroom cometh; go ye out to meet him.

Then all those virgins arose, and trimmed their lamps.

And the foolish said unto the wise, Give us of your oil; for our lamps are gone out.

But the wise answered, saying, Not so; lest there be not enough for us and you: but go ye rather to them that sell, and buy for yourselves.

And while they went to buy, the bridegroom came; and they that were ready went in with him to the marriage: and the door was shut.

Afterward came also the other virgins, saying, Lord, Lord, open to us.

But he answered and said, Verily I say unto you, I know you not.

Watch therefore, for ye know neither the day nor the hour wherein the Son of man cometh. (Matt. 25:2-13)

And another:

What man of you, having an hundred sheep, if he lose one of them, doth not leave the ninety and nine in the wilderness, and go after that which is lost, until he find it?

And when he hath found it, he layeth it on his shoulders, rejoicing.

And when he cometh home, he calleth together his friends and neighbors, saying unto them, Rejoice with me; for I have found my sheep which was lost.

I say unto you, that likewise joy shall be in heaven over one sinner that repenteth, more than over ninety and nine just persons, which need no repentance. (Luke 15:4-7)

If you were given the task of making known to the world that God cares enormously for one human life—no matter how wayward and wrong the life may be—how could you phrase a message more memorably than that? Yet how simple, how sincere, how splendidly crisp and direct! Benjamin Franklin in his autobiography tells the process which he went through in acquiring an effective style. He would read a passage from some great master of English, then lay the book aside and attempt to reproduce the thought in his own words. Comparing his version with the original, he discovered wherein he had obscured the thought or wasted words or failed to drive straight to the point. Every man who wishes to know a little more of Jesus should study the parables in the same fashion, schooling himself in their language and learning the elements of their power.

1. First of all they are marvelously condensed. Charles

A. Dana, it is reported, once issued an assignment to a new reporter on the *New York Sun*, directing him to confine his article to a column. The reporter protested that the story was too big to be compressed into so small a space.

"Get a copy of the Bible and read the first chapter of Genesis," said Dana. "You'll be surprised to find that the whole story of the creation of the world can be told in six hundred words."

Jesus had no introductions. A single sentence grips attention; three or four more tell the story; one or two more and both the thought and its application are clear. And this is true of ideas that reformed the moral structure of the world! When He wanted a new disciple, He said simply "Follow me." When He sought to explain the deepest philosophic mystery—the personality and character of God—He said, "A king made a banquet and invited many guests. God is that king and you are the guests; the Kingdom of Heaven is happiness—a banquet to be enjoyed."

Two men spoke on the battleground of Gettysburg nearly a century ago. The first delivered an oration of more than two hours in length; not one person in ten who reads this page can even recall his name; certainly not one in a thousand can quote a single sentence from his masterly effort. The second speaker uttered two hundred and fifty words, and those words, Lincoln's Gettysburg Address, are a part of the mental endowment of almost every American.

Many noble prayers have been sent up to the Throne of Grace—long impressive utterances. The prayer which Jesus taught His disciples consists of sixty-six words and can be written on the back of a post card. Many poems and essays have been penned by writers who hoped that they were making a permanent place for themselves in literature, but one of the greatest poems ever written consists of one hundred and eighty-eight words. It is the Twenty-third Psalm.

Jesus hated prosy dullness. He praised the Centurion who was anxious not to waste His time; the only prayer which He publicly commended was uttered by a poor publican who merely cried out, "God, be merciful to me a sinner." A seven-word prayer, and Jesus called it a good one. A sixty-six word prayer, He said, contained all that men needed to say or God to hear. What would be His verdict on most of our prayers and our speeches and our writing?

2. His language was marvelously simple—a second great essential. There is hardly a sentence in His teaching which a child cannot understand. His illustrations were all drawn from the commonest experiences of life: "a sower went forth to sow"; "a certain man had two sons"; "a man built his house on the sands"; "the kingdom of heaven is like a grain of mustard seed."

The absence of adjectives is striking. Henry Ward Beecher said once that "to a large extent adjectives are like leaves on a switch; they may make it look pretty, as a branch, but they prevent it striking tinglingly when you use it.

"I recollect a case in which my father at a public meeting was appointed to draw up an article," Beecher continued. "He had written one sentence: 'It is wrong.' Someone in the meeting got up and moved in his enthusiasm that this be corrected, and that the sentence read: 'It is exceedingly wrong.' My father got up and said, in his mild way, 'When I was writing out this resolution in its original shape that was the way I wrote it, but to make it stronger, I took out the "exceedingly." ' "

Jesus used few qualifying words and no long ones. We referred a minute ago to those three literary masterpieces. The Lord's Prayer, The Twenty-third Psalm, The Gettysburg Address. Recall their phraseology:

Our Father which art in Heaven, hallowed be
  thy name

The Lord is my shepherd; I shall not want

Four score and seven years ago

Not a single three-syllable word; hardly any two-syllable words. All the greatest things in human life are one-syllable things—love, joy, hope, home, child, wife, trust, faith, God—and the great pieces of writing, generally speaking, use the small word in place of the large if meaning permits.

3. Sincerity illuminates strongly every word, every sentence He uttered; sincerity is the third essential. Many wealthy men have purchased newspapers with the idea of advancing their personal fortunes or bringing about some political action in which they have a private interest. Such newspapers almost invariably fail. No matter how much money is spent on them, no matter how zealously the secret of their ownership is guarded, readers eventually become conscious that something is wrong. They come to feel that the voice of the editor is not his own.

It was the way Jesus looked at men, and the life He led among them, that gave His words transforming power. What He was and what He said were one and the same thing. Nobody could stand at His side for even a minute without being persuaded that here was a man who loved people and considered even the humblest of them worthy of the best He had to give. There is no presupposition more deadening to a writer than the idea that he can "write down" to his readers. No man was ever big enough to build enduringly on the basis of insincerity; but many like Peter the Hermit, fired with conviction, have been able to create and sustain a very considerable influence.

Jesus was notably tolerant of almost all kinds of sinners. He liked the companionship of the rough-and-ready folk who were entirely outside the churches; He was tender toward unfortunate women; He had a special fondness for James and John, whose ungovernable tempers had given them the title of "Sons of Thunder"; He forgave the weakness of Peter who denied Him; and He was not resentful at the unbelief of His near relatives and His native town. But for one sin He had no mercy. He denounced the insincerity of the Pharisees in phrases which sting like the lash of a whip. They thought they had a first mortgage on the Kingdom of Heaven, and He told them scornfully that only those who become like little children have any chance of entering in.

Little children know no pretense. They are startlingly frank. They look at the world through clear eyes and say only what they think. No writer, no orator, no salesman, exercises any large dominion in the world unless he can humble himself and partake of their nature.

"Though I speak with the tongues of men and of angels and have not charity, I am become as sounding brass or a tinkling cymbal," wrote Saint Paul.

Much brass has been sounded and many cymbals have tinkled in the presentation of ideas infinitely less complex and true. Persuasion depends on respect for the listeners, and in Jesus great respect coupled with great love.

4. Finally Jesus knew that any idea may have to be repeated.

One of the sons of James A. Garfield was traveling with his father through Ohio when the President was addressing county fairs. At the close of the day he asked the boy what he thought of his speeches.

The boy was embarrassed by the question. "Why...why

they were fine, Dad," he stammered, "but I felt uncomfortable part of the time. You repeated yourself so often; once you said the very same thing in different words four times over."

With a hearty laugh, Garfield slapped the boy's shoulder.

"So you thought your old dad was running out of ideas, did you?" he cried. "Well, I don't blame you; but there's a method in my madness. Tomorrow when I reach that passage in my talk, you watch the audience. The first time I make the point, you'll see by the faces that a few folks near the platform get it. But further back there will be noise and commotion; people will be turning their heads to find out who has just driven up, or what sort of hat Mrs. Jones has on, and they won't hear me at all. When I repeat it the first time a few faces in the middle of the crowd will show a response; on the third go, I'll make still more converts and on the fourth trial they'll all have a notion of what I am talking about. But it takes four shots to land them all; experience with all sorts of audiences has made me sure of that."

It has been said that "reputation is repetition." No important truth can be impressed on the minds of any large number of people by being said only once. The thoughts which Jesus had to give the world were revolutionary, but they were few in number. "God is your father," He said, "caring more for the welfare of every one of you than any human father can possibly care for his children. His Kingdom is happiness! His rule is love." This is what He had to teach, and He knew the necessity of driving it home from every possible angle. So in one of His stories God is the Shepherd searching the wilds for one wandering sheep; in another the Father welcoming home a prodigal boy; in another a King who forgives his debtors large amounts and expects them to be forgiving in turn—many stories but the same big Idea.

Because the stories were unforgettable, the idea lived and is today one of the most powerful influences on human action and thought. To be sure the work is far from complete. The idea that God is the Father of all men—not merely of a specially selected few—has still to reach some areas and to establish its dominance in society. More or less unconsciously a lot of us share the feeling of the French nobleman in Saint Simon's immortal story, who was sure that God would "think twice before damning a person of his quality."

Said the Duchess of Buckingham to the Countess of Huntingdon, in a delicious letter:

> I thank your Ladyship for the information concerning the Methodist preachers; their doctrines are most repulsive and strongly tinctured with impertinence and disrespect toward their superiors...It is monstrous to be told you have a heart as sinful as the common wretches that crawl on the earth. This is highly offensive and insulting, and I cannot but wonder that your Ladyship should relish any senti-

ments so much at variance with high rank and good breeding.

In spite of all the Duchesses of Buckingham, however, the great parables continue to advance. Monarchies are succeeded by democracies, building their governments on the firm foundation that men are free and equally entitled to a chance at the good things of life. The privileged protest and the agitators denounce, but slowly the world is learning.

And whoever feels an impulse to make his own life count in the grand process of human betterment can have no surer guide for his activities than Jesus. Let him learn the lesson of the parables: that in teaching people you first capture their interest; that your service rather than your sermons must be your claim on their attention; that what you say must be simple and brief and above all *sincere*—the unmistakable voice of true regard and affection.

"Ye," said He, "are my *friends*."

CHAPTER 6

HIS WAY IN OUR WORLD

WHEN JESUS was twelve years old, His father and mother took Him to the feast at Jerusalem.

It was the big national vacation; even peasant families saved their pennies and looked forward to it through the year. Towns like Nazareth were emptied of their inhabitants except for the few old people who were left behind to look after the very young ones. Crowds of cheerful pilgrims filled the highways, laughing on their way across the hills and under the stars at night.

In such a mass of people it was not surprising that a boy of twelve should be lost. When Mary and Joseph missed Him on the homeward trip, they took it calmly and began a search among the relatives.

The inquiry produced no result. Some remembered having seen Him in the Temple, but no one had seen

Him since. Mary grew frightened; where could He be? Back there in the city alone? Wandering hungry and tired through the friendless streets? Carried away by other travelers into a distant country? She pictured a hundred calamities. Nervously she and Joseph hurried back over the hot roads, through the suburbs, up through the narrow city streets, up to the courts of the Temple itself.

And there He was.

Not lost; not a bit worried. Apparently unconscious that the feast was over, He sat in the midst of a group of old men, who were questioning Him and applauding the common sense of His replies. Involuntarily His parents halted—they were simple folk, uneasy among strangers and disheveled by their haste. But after all they were His parents, and a very human feeling of irritation quickly overcame their diffidence.

Mary stepped forward and grasped His arm. "Son, why has thou thus dealt with us?" she demanded. "Behold, thy father and I have sought thee sorrowing."

I wonder what answer she expected to receive. Did she ever know exactly what He was going to say? Did anyone in Nazareth quite understand this keen eager lad who had such curious moments of abstraction and was forever breaking out with remarks that seemed far beyond His years?

He spoke to her now, with deference as always, but in words that did not dispel but rather added to her uncertainty.

"How is it that ye sought me?" He asked. "Wist ye not that I must be about my Father's business?"

Of course the anxious parents did not fully understand. Even if we consider they understood the boy's words as Luke is translated in the Revised Standard Version—"Did you not know I must be in my Father's house?"—we can imagine nothing but puzzlement. A prosperous carpenter shop was exactly the place for the boy.

Yet Mary said nothing more. Something in His look and tone silenced her. She and Joseph turned and started out, and Jesus followed them—away from the Temple and the city back to little Nazareth. Luke tells it with a grave and beautiful simplicity. "And he went down with them, and came to Nazareth, and was subject unto them; but his mother kept all these sayings in her heart."

His hour of boyish triumph had not turned His head. He knew how thorough must be His preparation. A building can rise high into the air only as it has sunk its foundations deep into the earth; the part of a man's life which the world sees is effective in proportion as it rests on solid foundations never seen. He knew this. For eighteen years more He was content to remain in the little town—until His strength was mature; until He had done His full duty by His mother and the younger children. Until His hour had come. "And Jesus increased in wisdom and stature, and in favour with God and man."

But what interests us most in this one recorded incident of His boyhood is that He defined here and at this age the purpose of His career. He did not say, "Wist ye not that I must show men the range of my understanding?" or "Wist ye not that I must get ready to meet the arguments of men like these?" The language and intent were quite different. However we translate, the essential remains the same. Here He announced to men His dedication. We know what followed. Thus we understand what those who first heard could not. He was saying that, obedient to God's will, He offered His life to men. To what extent is this principle by which He conducted His life applicable to ours? And if He were among us again in a time again tormented by selfishness, ambition, pride and misunderstanding, would His philosophy work?

Before we consider that let's turn to another occasion when, you recall, He stated more fully the great principle.

It was on the afternoon when James and John came to ask Him what promotion they might expect. They were two of the most energetic of the lot, called "Sons of Thunder" by the rest, being noisy and always in the middle of some sort of storm. They had joined the ranks because they liked Him, but they had no very definite idea of what it was all about. Now they wanted to know where the enterprise was heading and just what there would be in it for them.

"Master," they said, "we want to ask what plans you have in mind for us. You're going to need strong men around you when you establish your kingdom; our ambition is to sit on either side of you, one on your right hand and the other on your left."

Can we really object to that attitude? Each of us has asked or hoped for advancement. If we want a better place, we usually ask for it.

Jesus answered with a sentence of great poetry. But wouldn't it have sounded absurd to the sons of thunder?

"Whosoever will be great among you, shall be your minister," He said, "and whosoever of you will be the chiefest, shall be servant of all." And He added that He had come "not to be ministered unto but to minister..."

Grand sounding, yes. But isn't it contradictory? Be a good servant and you will be great; be the best possible servant and you will occupy the highest possible place. A splendid speech but utterly impractical; nothing to take seriously in a common-sense world. That is just what most men thought century after century; and then, quite suddenly, great enterprises—science, industry, business services—woke up to a great discovery. For several decades now that discovery has been proclaimed more and more widely and frequently as something distinctly modern.

Free men, acting independently of government, pool their skills and money to aid other men in other countries who have been enslaved. The wealth of a family or a corporation is put to work in the service of science, the arts, education.

The principle that he who serves best accomplishes

most spreads to every area. I observe most closely what is closest to me, and I know that business and industry have learned that a real understanding of and regard for the individual and the social or business community, large or small, must be part of every aspect of work. The huge plants and financial strength of, say, an automobile manufacturer rest on the willingness and ability not only to provide for your safety, comfort and convenience but to feel—and convince you of it—a genuine concern for your pleasure in the product, your benefit from it.

Of course the manufacturer has a profit motive. But to say that as if it made the service a mere sales trick is to misread the record and miss the point entirely. Some self-interest (not selfishness) can be shown in almost any human enterprise, and it may well be a vital worthy part of most. The important fact is that we seem to be increasing our awareness that worthiness is related to any advancement or gain.

The evidence of this new attitude is overwhelming. Manufacturers of building equipment, of clothes, of food; presidents of railroads and steamship companies; the heads of banks and investment houses—all of them tell the same story. They call it the "spirit of modern business"; they suppose, most of them, that it is something very new. Jesus preached it more than nineteen hundred years ago.

One afternoon in a Pullman car I listened to a wise man who certainly understood what Jesus was saying to James and John.

"I am amazed by some of the young men who ask me to use my influence to get them better positions or increases in salary," he said. "Such an attitude on their part shows an absolute failure to understand fundamentals. I spent many years in one business, with one company. I never once asked what my salary or title was to be. None of the men who made that company ever wasted time over such questions. We had a vision of extending our company's service throughout the world, of making it the finest, must useful institution of its kind." True, the company made this gentlemen rich. My own conviction is that he thought of service, not of gain if he served.

"If you're forever thinking about saving your life," Jesus said, "you'll lose it; but the man who loses his life shall find it."

Because He said it and He was a religious teacher, because it's printed in the Bible, does it fail to apply in any way to a man's work? What did the man on the Pullman mean if it wasn't that he and his friends buried themselves in a great undertaking, literally lost their lives in it? And when they found their lives again, they were all of them bigger and richer in all ways that they had ever supposed they could be. Would they have achieved so much if they had been careful and calculating about themselves? "We mustn't overdo this thing," they might have said. "This is a good company and deserves to grow, but every man must look out for his own interests. Just what is there going to be in it for us?" Instead they worked selflessly to build something they considered good and useful. Does the financial reward make worthless the dedication that never had this profit in view?

One spring morning the founder of a great manufacturing company tipped a kitchen chair back against the wall and asked me: "Have you ever noticed that the man who starts out in life with a determination to make money never makes very much?"

It was rather a startling question, and without waiting for my comment he went on to answer it. "When we were building our original model, do you suppose that it was money we were thinking about? Of course we expected that it would be profitable if it succeeded, but that wasn't in the front of our minds. We wanted to make our product so inexpensive that every family in the United States could afford to have one. So we worked morning, noon and night, until our muscles ached and our nerves were ragged. One night when we were almost at the breaking point I said to the boys, 'Well, there's one consolation. Nobody can deliver more for less if he's not willing to work harder than we've worked.' And so far," he concluded with a whimsical smile, "nobody has been willing to do that."

Though it happened long ago I'll never forget one trip from Chicago to New York on the Twentieth Century Limited. We were due at Grand Central Station at nine-forty, a nice leisurely hour, and three of us who were traveling together decided to make a comfortable morning of it. We got out of our berths at a quarter after eight, shaved and dressed and half an hour later were making our way back to the dining car.

A door to one of the drawing rooms was open, and as we walked by we could hardly keep from looking in. The bed in the room had been made up long since; a table stood between the windows, and at the table, buried in work, was a man whose face the newspapers had made familiar to everyone. He had been Governor of New York, a Justice of the Supreme Court, a candidate for the Presidency of the United States.

My companions and I were young men; he was well along in middle life. We were unknown; he was famous. We were doing all that was required of us. We were up and dressed and would be ready for work when the train pulled in at a little before ten. But this man, of whom nothing was actually required, was doing far more. I thought to myself as we passed on to our leisurely breakfast, "That explains him; now I understand how he has done what he has done."

"And whosoever shall compel thee to go a mile," Jesus said, "go with him twain."

Which, as I understand it, means, "Do more than is required of you, do twice as much." Another startling bit of advice. Where will a man ever get if he delivers twice as much as he is expected or paid to do? The answer is that he will probably succeed in whatever he is doing.

Here is another principle, seemingly equally impracticable.

Remember the words of Jesus when He said, "It is more blessed to give than to receive."

We came perilously near to losing those words. They are not recorded in any one of the four Gospels. Matthew, Mark, Luke and John did not set them down. Of course we don't know why. Yet it's possible to believe that even to these devoted men the words must have seemed to contradict all experience. At any rate they all passed over the saying. But Paul did not. He who had abandoned a social position and an assured career for the service of the Galilean, he who had already given so much and would later give his life, *he* heard the words and remembered. He understood.

Are they empty words? Is a man a fool to let them be a guiding influence in his life? I talked one day with a great historian. I said:

"You have stood upon a mountain and viewed the whole panorama of human progress. You have seen the captains and kings, the princes and the prophets, the scientists and the adventurers, the millionaires and the dreamers. What heads rise above the common level? Among all those who have fought for fame, *who* have actually achieved it? What half dozen men among them all deserve to be called great?"

He turned the questions over in his mind for a day or two, and then gave a list of six names, with his reasons for each. An extraordinary list!

Jesus of Nazareth

Buddha

Asoka

Aristotle

Roger Bacon

Abraham Lincoln

Think of the thousands of emperors who have battled for fame, who have decreed themselves immortal and fashioned their immortality into monuments of brick and stone. Yet Asoka, who ruled in India centuries before Christ, is the only emperor on the list, and he is there not because of his victories but because he voluntarily abandoned war and devoted himself to the betterment of his millions of subjects. Think of the hosts who have struggled for wealth, fretting over figures, denying their generous instincts, cheating and grasping and worrying. But no millionaire is on the list, with the exception again of Asoka. Who sat on the throne in Rome when Jesus of Nazareth hung on the cross? Who ruled the hosts of Persia when Aristotle thought and taught? Who was King of England when Roger Bacon laid the foundations of modern scientific research?

And when the historian, looking over the field where they contended for the prize, seeks for something which has endured, he finds the message of a teacher, the dream of a scientist, the vision of a seer. "These six men stood on the corners of history," the historian said. "Events hinged on them. The current of human thought was freer and clearer because they had lived and worked. They took little from the world and left it much. They did not get; they gave and, in the giving, gained eternal influence."

In our own country, in Monticello, Virginia, an American statesman lies buried. He was Secretary of State, Minister to France, President of the United States. His epitaph makes reference to none of these honors. It reads:

> Here was buried
> Thomas Jefferson
> Author
> of the Declaration of American Independence
> of the Statute of Virginia
> for Religious Freedom
> and Father of the
> University of Virginia

The offices that he held are forgotten on the stone. He desired to be remembered only by what he gave. And he has his wish.

Somewhere in his *Essays* Emerson has a sentence to this effect: "See how the mass of men worry themselves into nameless graves, while here and there a great unselfish soul forgets himself into immortality." It is a fine thought, finely phrased, but Jesus thought it first.

So we have the main points of His philosophy:

1. Whoever will be great must render great service.
2. Whoever will find himself at the top must be willing to lose himself at the bottom.
3. The rewards come to those who travel the second, undemanded mile.

Judas would have sneered at all this. Not really a bad fellow at heart, he had the virtues and the weaknesses of the small-bore businessman. He was hard-boiled, and proud of it; he "looked out for Number One." It was no easy job being treasurer for a lot of idealists, Judas would have you know. He held the bag and gave every cent a good tight squeeze before he let it pass. When the grateful woman broke her box of costly ointment over Jesus' feet, the other disciples thought it was fine, but Judas knew better. "Pretty wasteful business," he grumbled to himself. The big talk of the others about "thrones" and "kingdoms" and "victory" did not fool him; he could read a balance sheet, and he knew that the jig was up. So he made his private little deal with the priests, probably supposing that Jesus would be arrested, reproved and warned not to preach in Jerusalem again. "I will get mine and retire," he said to himself.

But Jesus said, "I, if I be lifted up [on the cross; that is to say, if I lose my life] will draw all men to me." Each made his decision and received his reward.

We have spoken of a few men and a few pursuits, but the same sound principles apply to every walk of life. Great progress will be made in the world when we rid ourselves of the idea that there is a difference between work and religious work. We have been taught that a man's daily business activities are selfish, and that only the time which he devotes to church meetings and social service activities can be sincerely dedicated to accomplishing good. Ask any ten people what Jesus meant by His "Father's business," and nine of them will answer "preaching," To interpret the words in this narrow sense is to lose the real significance of His life. It was not to preach that He came into the world—nor to teach nor to heal. These are all aspects of His Father's business, but the business itself is far larger, more inclusive. For if human life has any significance, it is this—that God has set going here an experiment to which all His resources are committed. He seeks to develop perfect human beings, superior to circumstance, victorious over fate. No single kind of human talent or effort can be spared if the experiment is to succeed. The race must be fed and clothed and housed and transported, as well as preached to and taught and healed. All work *can* be worship; all useful service prayer. And whoever works wholeheartedly at any worthy calling associates himself with the Almighty in the great enterprise which He has initiated but which can never be finished until men do their full part.

How does a man achieve? What constitutes "success"? Jesus spoke of crowns and died on a cross. He talked of His kingdom, and ended His days amid the jeers and taunts of His enemies. "He was in all points tempted like as we are," says the Epistle to the Hebrews. We have read it often, heard it read oftener, but we have never believed it, of course...The conception of His character which some theologians have given us makes any such idea impossible. He was born differently from the rest of us, they insist. He did not belong among us at all, but came down from Heaven on a brief visit, spent a few years in reproving men for their mistakes, died and went back to Heaven again. A hollow bit of stage play. What chance for temptation in such a career? How can an actor go wrong when his whole part is written and learned in advance?

It is frightfully hard to free the mind from the numbing grip of long-established attitudes. But let us make the effort. Let us touch once more the great episodes in this finest, most exalted story, considering now the perils and crises of success in its truest sense.

Jesus was not at all sure where He was going when He laid down His tools and turned His back on the carpenter shop—unless we can believe this, His struggle ceases to be "in all points" like our own; for each of us has to venture on life as onto an uncharted sea. Something inside Him carried Him forward—the something which has whispered to so many boys that there is a place for them in the world which lies beyond the hills. He went to John to be baptized and for a while John's influence molded Him. He, too, retired into the wilderness and there met the *first* crisis of His career. When He emerged,

He had formed His own plan for His work; asceticism and denunciation, He knew, were not the role for Him.

His first success was swift beyond all expectations. Out of the Temple, shrieking and cursing, went the money-changers, while the crowd cheered His name until it echoed. That night the whole city was stirred. When He left, at the end of the feast, and went back into His own north country, He found that His fame had preceded Him. Crowds flocked to hear Him talk; news of His deeds of healing traveled ahead of Him everywhere. His vision of His work began to take definite shape. He would restore the self-respect of the people, abolishing the rule of formalism, and establishing a fresh, glorious conception of the Fatherhood of God and the brotherhood of man. It all seemed so natural, so easy, there in the warm sunshine of Galilee with the responsive faces of the multitude turned eagerly toward Him. The year or year and a half that followed were filled with the joy of increasing reputation and achievement. Apparently there was not a single cloud in the sky.

But there were people in Jerusalem with whose private affairs His ideas would seriously interfere. He was not left long in doubt as to their attitude. Incensed at His cleansing of the Temple, they sent their spies into the north country to report His movements, and they made every effort to turn the crowds away. Perhaps at first He had hope of winning even His enemies to His teaching—so altogether simple and satisfying His message seemed to

Him. If so, the hope soon vanished. Opposition crystallized; it made itself felt in every audience He addressed, in every town He visited. Reluctantly He had to face the fact that the time was coming when He must compromise or fight. It was with this realization that He faced a second and a greater crisis.

He had crossed the lake one day in a little boat to get away from the crowds, but they were too quick for Him. They hurried around the end of the lake, gathering recruits as they went, and waited for Him at the landing place—more that five thousand strong. He was tired and wanted a chance to rest and think. But there were the people, pathetically eager, and He "had compassion on them." So He sat down among them and went on with His teaching until the day was almost over. Then, at last, the disciples came, hardly concealing their tired petulance, and demanded that He send them away.

"But they have made a long trip and have been with us all day without food," He replied. "We must feed them before they go."

The disciples regarded Him with blank amazement.

"Feed them—on what?" they demanded, "We have no money, and even if we had there are more than five thousand in the crowd!"

Jesus apparently did not hear them.

"Have them sit down," He commanded. "Gather up whatever food you can find and bring it here to me."

Doubtingly, but too well-trained to argue, the disciples

did as they were told. They arranged the crowd in companies of fifty and a hundred, collected the little supply of food which the more prudent members had brought, and laid the collection at His feet. He lifted His eyes to Heaven, blessed the food, ordered it redistributed and somehow the people ate and were satisfied.

Just what happened in the moment when the food was laid before Him is an impenetrable mystery, but there is no doubt at all as to what took place afterward. It was the event for which the people had waited, the unmistakable sign! Moses had fed their fathers on manna in the wilderness; here was one who likewise called on Heaven and supplied their wants. Surely He was the son of David, long foretold, who would overthrow the rule of their conquerors and restore the throne to Jerusalem!

Joyously they shouted the news back and forth. The day of deliverance had come; the tyranny of the Romans was about to end. Their enthusiasm carried them to their feet—fifty in this group, a hundred in that; almost as if by magic they found themselves organized. They were an army and had not realized it. Right there on the field they were enough to outnumber the garrison in Jerusalem; but they were only a nucleus of the host that would gather to their banners, once their southward march was formed. If they were five thousand now, they would be fifty thousand, perhaps a hundred thousand then. A wild enthusiasm seized them. Shouting His name at the top of their voices, they surged forward toward the little hill where He stood...

And then—

He had foreseen their purpose, and even while they were perfecting their plan, doubt had raged through His spirit with the force of a tempest. Why not accept their nomination? Why not be their king? It would mean an alteration in His program, to be sure—a surrender of His vision of spiritual leadership. And yet it might not be such a surrender, after all. Solomon had been king, and a great spiritual leader; David had been king and had written the nation's highest ideals into his Psalms. He Himself was better balanced than David, wiser than Solomon—why not?

It was a splendid a picture as ever stirred the pulses of an ambitious man. For only an instant Jesus allowed His eyes to rest on it. Then He saw the other picture—the vast dumb multitudes of men, His brothers and sisters, the blind being led by the blind, their souls squeezed dry of vision and hope by the machinery of formalism. He saw generations born and die in spiritual servitude which nothing could end except the Truth that He had come to declare. To put Himself at the head of this army of fanatical patriots would be perhaps to risk His life and His message with it. But worse than the possibility of failure was the probability of success. To be king of the Jews would mean a lifetime spent in the defense of His throne and title, a lifetime of bloodshed and intrigue, while His message remained unspoken. Living, He would give His people only a semblance of national life; eventually He would die and leave them to be re-enslaved by the Roman power. And the Truth which He had come to declare, which was capable of continuing its work of emancipation throughout the world as long as time should last, would be traded for a glittering crown and an empty name. In a flash He saw it all and made His decision. Even as the multitude surged forward, He gave a few crisp orders to his disciples and disappeared.

The Gospel story puts the dramatic climax into a single sentence:

> When Jesus therefore perceived that they would come and take him by force, to make him a king, he departed again into a mountain himself alone. (John 6:15)

In that hour of crisis He proved His title to be the companion, guide and master of every man and woman in every time. His understanding was universal. There is no worthy work of mind or muscle that cannot lead to Him, that does not inherit from Him its most valid charter and most useful policy.

There is no mere theorizing in His words; He speaks out of what He Himself has proved. If He says that a man's work is more eternally important than any title, He has a right to speak. He Himself refused the highest title. If He says that there are things more vital than merely making money, let no one question His authority. He was handed the wealth of a nation and handed it back again. Idealist He is, but there is nothing in the whole hard world so practical as His ideals. "There is a success which is greater than wealth or titles," He says. "It comes through making your work an instrument of greater service and larger living to your fellow men and women. This is my Father's business and He needs your help."

He told one story which should be published every year in all business magazines, all trade papers, all house organs. It concerned a certain rich man whose enterprises prospered beyond all his expectations. His hand "brought forth plentifully," so much that he said to himself: "What shall I do, because I have no room where to bestow my fruits?"

> And he said, This will I do: I will pull down my barns and build greater; and there will I bestow all my fruits and my goods.
> And I will say to my soul, Soul, thou hast much goods laid up for many years; take thine ease, eat, drink, and be merry.
> But God said unto him, Thou, fool, this night thy soul shall be required of thee...
> (Luke 12:18-20)

The poor fool had regarded his business as nothing but a means of escape from business. He had hoarded his wealth, denying every generous impulse; spent his health, forfeiting every chance for wholesome enjoyment; sacrificed the joy of living for selfish satisfaction that he hoped was coming when he had made his pile. And fate laughed in his face. He thought he had provided for every contingency, but the one great event which is always unexpected came like a thief and found him unprepared...

With that anecdote should be published another, which is also a tragedy. It concerns the little hotel in Bethlehem, "the inn."

The mother of Jesus of Nazareth knocked at its doors and could not come in. It might have sheltered the greatest event in human history, and it lost its chance.

Why? Why was Jesus born in a stable? Because the people in the inn were vicious or hostile? Not in the least. The inn was full, that was all; every room was taken by folk who had affairs to attend to and money to spend. It was busy.

There was no "room in the inn."

Men's lives are sometimes like that inn.

You know a man whose heart is broken because his son is a fool. Yet deep within himself he knows that the fault is his own. All through the formative years of the boy's development, he never gave him any time. Not that he didn't love the boy, but he was busy. There was no room for family life, and his son is a fool.

You know men whose health is gone; men whose taste for reading and music and art is gone. Men who have literally no interests in life beyond the office which has become a mere treadmill on which their days are ground away.

In the process of being successful they have sacrificed success. Never once forgetting themselves, they have forgotten everything else. This is not Jesus' idea of what a life should be. He, who refused to turn aside from His business to become a king, was never too busy to turn aside for a sick man, a friend, a little child. He never forgot that one night His mother had stood on a threshold where there was no welcome.

The threshold of the little inn in Bethlehem. It was so busy that the greatest event in history knocked at its doors—

and could not come in.

Chapter 7

The Master

So we come to the end. To the final tests of a man's living...
How does he bear disappointment?
How does he die?

For two years it seemed almost certain that Jesus would prevail. We have marked the dramatic success with which His work began. We have watched the crowds flock about Him in the market place; we have heard the cheers that greeted His victories over shrewd antagonists and the murmured awe when a sick man rose and walked. Reports of His triumphs preceded Him everywhere so that men competed for the honor of being His host, there was friendliness in His audiences that made almost anything seem possible. And why not? If, by accepting His message, men could be lifted up, transformed into sons of God, heirs of eternity, why should any be so stubborn or so foolish as to oppose? Surely such truth must conquer.

If you read the story carefully, you can see how His tone and manner grew in confidence. In hours of exalted communion He stood face to face with God, felt Himself God's son, knew that He could lift the hearts of men as no other had ever lifted them. The knowledge thrilled Him beyond ecstasy. "I am the Way," He cried, and He called on His friends to free themselves, to cast their burdens upon the Lord, to believe more, rejoice more, *expect* more of God.

Those who listened in those days were profoundly impressed. Even the most callous yielded grudging admiration. "Never man so spake," said they. As for the multitude, its enthusiasm would brook no halfway measures. They would take Him by force and make Him king.

Then came the change.

His home town was first to turn against Him. Picture, if you will, the enthusiasm with which He planned His visit to it. Nazareth was little and despised, a jest among the wits of the day. It had produced no great men, been the scene of no historic achievement. Jesus knew all this. Those familiar streets and faces must often have been in His memory. When He healed a sick man in Capernaum, it could well have pleased Him to think that the report would be carried back to Nazareth. When He drove the plunderers from the Temple, He might have realized that, in the fame which had come to Him, His home town would have a share. "Jesus of Nazareth," His world called

Him, linking its name with His. He had lifted the little village out of obscurity. And now, in the height of His glory, He was going back.

Did He arrive in the dusk and slip almost unnoticed through the streets to His mother's house? Perhaps she was in the kitchen; on hearing that footstep which she could never mistake, she ran and threw her arms around His neck.

"Jesus," she cried, patting His cheek and looking up at Him with glistening eyes. "Jesus, my boy, my boy!"

Hearing the name His brothers and sisters came hurrying from other parts of the house. All sorts of reports had drifted back—almost unbelievable reports. Every day the gossips of the village had stopped them to ask whether a letter or a message had come.

"Seems to be doing great things," said the gossips with ill-concealed envy. "Hope He doesn't try to go too far," they said in tones which revealed all too clearly their real hope that He *would* go too far and come to grief.

Against cynicism and innuendo, we can believe His brothers had stood their ground proudly. He *was* doing great things. The reports were not a bit exaggerated. Someday He would come back and show them all; the townspeople would wish then that they had believed...And now He was back. He looked healthy and confident, but not otherwise different. Nazareth was a bit disappointed and He felt it. People, we reason, hardly knew what it was. Perhaps they had expected that He would be somehow bigger or better dressed or tagged with some outward sign of authority...With forced enthusiasm they bustled about, asking Him questions, praising His appearance, but through it all ran a note of restraint.

"Come now, you must get to bed early," His mother may have said. "They will all be wanting to see you at the synagogue tomorrow."

So He went up to the room, His old room, alone. The homecoming was not quite what He had dreamed. They loved Him; they were proud of Him, but they doubted—that was clear enough. And they dreaded the test that must come next day.

He awoke refreshed and heartened. Some neighbors dropped in after breakfast, for the report of His arrival had spread quickly through the little town. When He and His mother reached the door of the synagogue, a crowd was waiting outside. They returned His greeting with a mixture of regard and curiosity and pushed promptly through the door behind Him, filling the little room. There was much whispering and craning of necks. He made His way to the front of the room, picked up the roll of the prophet Isaiah, turned around toward them and smiled.

Instantly all His illusions vanished. Instead of sympathetic understanding there was only cynicism on those faces. The old woman, His neighbor, whom He had planned to heal, was sitting prominently in front. She was willing to take a chance on anything, for she had been a long time sick, but her look was less a hope than a

challenge. The substantial men of the town settled solidly in their appointed seats, and dared Him with their hard
eyes to try His tricks on *them*! "You may have caused a stir
in Capernaum," they seemed to say, "but Nazareth isn't
so slow. We know you. You're no prophet; you're just the
son of Joseph the carpenter, and you can't fool us!"

Slowly He opened the roll, and in tones that stirred
them in spite of themselves He began to read:

> The Spirit of the Lord is upon me, because he
> hath anointed me to preach the gospel to the
> poor; he hath sent me to heal the brokenheart-
> ed, to preach deliverance to the captives, and
> recovering of sight to the blind, to set at liberty
> them that are bruised,
> To preach the acceptable year of the Lord.
> (Luke 4:18-19)

He closed the book and handed it back to the atten-
dant. "This day is this Scripture fulfilled in your ears," He
said simply. There was an ominous silence in the synagogue. "And the eyes of all...were fastened on him." He
knew what they were thinking; they wanted Him to do
some such mighty work as He had done in Capernaum.
But He knew, He must have known, also the uselessness
of trying. Scorn and ignorant self-sufficiency were mira-
cle-proof. They would never receive Him, never be proud
of Him. They merely wanted Him to exhibit Himself and

they hoped that He would fail. "No prophet is accepted in his own country," He said to them sadly. Elisha before Him had said, "Neither is this the city." With a look of soul weariness He turned to leave.

Then the storm broke. All the pent-up envy of the little town for one who had dared to outgrow it burst out. The townsmen roared and surged forward, hurrying Him through the main street to the edge of a precipice where they would have thrown Him over. But the wrath which had been sufficient to conceive His destruction grew suddenly impotent when He turned and faced them. They shrank back, and before they could re-form their purpose, He had passed "through the midst of them" and was on His way. In His ears sounded the buzz of malicious comment, but He was too heart-sick to look back. From henceforth Capernaum became "his own city." Nazareth, the home of His youth, the dwelling place of His boyhood friends and neighbors, had given its verdict.

He had come unto His own, and His own received Him not.

His brothers deserted Him. We ought not to blame them too much perhaps. No man is a hero to his valet. The close relatives of any great man, who have lived with him through the familiar experiences of everyday life, must be always a little mystified by the world's worship. The brothers of Jesus had been witnesses of His defeat, and were left behind by Him to bear the ignominy of it. How the sardonic laughter must have rung in their ears! How endlessly the wits must have cracked their jokes about that morning in the synagogue...These home-town sneers were bad enough, but the reports that came back from other towns threw the simple unimaginative family into a panic. It was said that He made seditious speeches; that He claimed to have a special relationship to God; that He utterly disregarded the Code of the Pharisees and denounced them openly before the crowds. Such conduct could mean only one thing. He would get Himself into jail, and His relatives with Him. Hence, the members of His family, who should have been His best helpers, spent their energy in the effort to get Him to go further away from home. Once when the Feast of Tabernacles was being celebrated in Jerusalem, they urged Him to "depart hence" and taunted Him, saying that if He could really do all that He claimed, the place for Him to make His reputation was at the capital. Anything to get Him out of Galilee. They were all unsafe while He stayed near them—so they thought.

"For neither did his brethren believe in him."
(John 7:5)

He was teaching one day in Capernaum, to a crowd that hung spellbound on his words, when suddenly an interruption occurred. A messenger pushed through the audience to tell Him that His mother and brothers were outside and insisted on speaking to Him right away. A quick look of pain shot across His face. He knew why they had come; they had been sending Him hints of their coming for weeks. They had made up their minds that He was just a little bit out of His head, and they were determined His extravagances should not ruin them all. He drew Himself up to His full height and pointing to His disciples turned to the messenger:

"My mother and brethren?" He repeated. "Behold those who believe on me, *they* are my mother and my brethren."

They *were* indeed His real kindred, and many times they proved themselves worthy of the name; but even their devotion could not entirely remove the hurt. When later He had His brief hour of triumph, when the crowds flung their garments into the streets before Him and shouted their "Hosannas," even then His heart must have been sore at the thought that in all that multitude there was not one of the brothers for whom He had sacrificed so much of His youth. A warm hand clasp from one of them would have meant more than all the high homage of the multitude. But they were far away, still ashamed of the relationship, still regarding Him as well meaning but not quite sane.

His best friend died doubting Him. To that friend, John the Baptist, He owed His initial success. John had introduced Him to the people; His first disciples had come because John pointed Him out as a greater prophet than he himself. The two men were entirely unlike in character and method. John was austere, harsh, denunciatory—a lonely spirit, dwelling apart. Jesus was cheerful, friendly, never happier than when in a crowd. John laid down for his disciples a rigid program of ceremonies and fasts; Jesus disregarded forms and encouraged His disciples to disregard them. He recognized that He and John must do their work in different ways, but it had not occurred to Him that their differences would ever loosen the bond of friendship. He was cut to the quick, therefore, when two messengers came from John with a wistful, doubting question:

"Are you *really* a prophet, as I told people that you are?" John asked. "Instead of fasting, you banquet. Instead of calling on men to abjure pleasure, you share their pleasures. Are you the hope of the world, as I believed you to be, or must we look for another?"

Very tenderly, but sadly, Jesus sent back His reply. "Go tell John what you have seen and heard," He said, "how the blind see, lepers are cleansed and the poor have the good news preached to them."

It was a wonderful answer, but did it convince His friend? A few weeks later, in the dungeon of Herod's castle, John paid a last great penalty for his idealism and courage. Jesus, when He heard of it, "withdrew into a desert place alone." His closest friend and first adherent had been killed—a sacrifice to the selfishness of a social order which He Himself was fighting. In that heartbreaking event He saw an omen for Himself. They who had been strong enough to murder John would one day destroy Him also. When He returned, there was a new seriousness in His face, a harder note in His teachings. He saw at the end of His path the shadow of the cross. And His heart was heavy because the friend who ought to have understood Him best had misunderstood Him and died in doubt.

The people deserted Him. When last we caught a glimpse of them, they were cheering His name beside the lake, seeking to force Him to be their king. He eluded them and retired into the mountain to think and pray. It must have been a dramatic moment when He reappeared. Only a single "Yes" was needed, and they would have lifted Him on their shoulders and borne Him in triumph to the city gates. Hushed and expectant they waited for His answer—and what an answer! "I am not come to restore the kingdom to Jerusalem," He cried. "Mine is a spiritual mission: I am the bread of life. You have cheered me because I fed you in the wilderness, but I tell you now that what I have come to give you is myself, that by knowing me you may know your Father."

They could not have been more stunned if He had struck their leaders across the face. What did He mean by this senseless mysticism, this talk about "the bread of life"? Hadn't they seen Him heal the sick and conquer the Pharisees in debate—were not these signs that He was the leader, so long promised, who would rout the Romans and restore the throne of David? And now, when the hour was ripe, when they were ready to march, why this language which nobody could understand?

The Jews therefore murmured concerning Him, because He said, "I am the bread that came down from Heaven." It was sacrilege or nonsense, one or the other. In either event it proved Him an unsound leader. Gentiles might continue to follow Him if they chose, but His company was clearly no place for a self-respecting Jew.

Silently the cautious people slipped away, and afterward denied that they had ever had anything to do with Him. Those who were more daring or devoted continued with Him through the rest of the week, and on the Sabbath crowded into the synagogue where they knew that He would speak. The days had given Him time to reconsider and compose His thoughts; perhaps now He would make a reasonable reply to their hopes. But there was no compromise in His message that day. Again He repeated His seemingly senseless talk about the "bread of life." It destroyed the last hope of those who had looked to Him for the deliverance of Israel. "These are hard sayings," they protested, "who can understand them?"

And then the note of tragedy. *"Upon this many of his disciples went back and walked with him no more."* So Saint John notes in his Gospel the faithlessness of the crowds that had professed faith.

The tide had turned. He realized it clearly though the twelve could not. At every opportunity He sought to build up in them an increased sense of their responsibilities. He must "go into Jerusalem," He told them, "and suffer many things of the elders and chief priests and scribes, and be killed." They could not, would not believe it. Peter, hotheaded and enthusiastic, took Him aside and rebuked Him for what seemed a temporary loss of courage. "Be it far from thee, Lord," he exclaimed; "this shall never be unto thee." Generous loyal words, but they revealed an utter failure to appreciate the real situation. All hope of a revived and regenerated nation was gone; Jesus' one chance now for permanent influence was in welding His little group closer together and sealing their union with His blood.

For the first time in His public work He forsook Palestine and led His wondering but still dutiful followers into the foreign cities of Tyre and Sidon. The journey gave Him a chance to be alone with the twelve; and it was, in a small way, a repetition of His earlier triumphs. These foreign folk were friendly without ulterior motive. They cared nothing about the establishment of a throne in Jerusalem or the possibility of profit for themselves from His political triumph. They came to hear Him because His words thrilled them, because they felt their better selves touched and made vibrant by the wonder of His life.

He hated to leave these kindly strangers. Much more He dreaded the thought of another trip through Galilee. What a graveyard of high hopes it was! Every road, every street corner, almost every house and tree was alive with memories of His earlier triumphs. Now He must pass each one again, conscious that it might be the last time, His heart weighed down with the thought of high purposes that had brought no response and sacrifices seemingly in vain. Small wonder that He cried out against Chorazin and Bethsaida and even His own loved Capernaum, the cities for which He had done so much. "Woe unto you," He cried in His loneliness, "for if the mighty works which were done in you had been done in Tyre and Sidon they would have repented long ago, in sackcloth and ashes."

But neither Bethsaida nor Capernaum had ears for Him now. Some other novelty had taken hold of the public imagination. He had had His day; nothing more was to be expected from Him. So the spring and summer passed, and autumn came, bringing the Feast of Tabernacles, which He determined to celebrate in Jerusalem. It was a suicidal resolve. The report of His dwindling influence had been carried to the Temple clique, which was emboldened by the information. There were spies in every crowd that listened to Him; the echo of His smallest act was heard in the capital; He could not hope to arrive outside the city walls without imminent danger of arrest. All this He knew, but it did not weigh against His resolve. This might be His last feast. There would be visitors from all over the world, some of whom would surely take the seed of His message with them back to their homes. He must be true to His calling at whatever cost. So He went.

We catch one glimpse of Him on the Temple steps, surrounded by a partly curious, partly antagonistic crowd. It was His chance to recapture a little of the popular favor, to speak a placating word that might open the way to reconciliation; but no such thought entered His mind. The time for defiance had come. "I have offered you the truth," He cried, "the truth that would make you free." And when they shouted that they were sons of Abraham and hence already free, He replied that they were no children of Abraham, but "children of the devil."

They would have killed Him then and there, but their courage failed. After all He had still a considerable following, and it was better to wait. Give Him rope and He would tangle Himself inextricably. Every speech was alienating somebody. When the time was ripe, they would seize Him—perhaps at the next feast, if in the meantime He had not entirely discredited Himself and disappeared. So they argued among themselves, and He went back once more into His Galilee.

Just for a moment, in the next spring, there seemed to be a renewed popular interest. The crowds flocked around in the old familiar way; the disciples noted it joyously. "The multitudes come together to Him again," they exclaimed and at once their hopes were busy with new visions of His success. But dismay followed fast. Against their ardent protest He carried them off into close retirement. They were restless, lonely, distressed at the way in which He turned away supporters. Was it necessary to be so harsh with the Pharisees? After all there were many estimable men among them whose contributions would have been very helpful. Why should He have ridiculed them? Why tell people that their precious ritual was less acceptable to God than the cry for mercy of an untaught publican? Why slight their ready hospitality in favor of an outcast like Zacchaeus? His little group of friends were still groping for a clear vision of message and purposes when for the last time He led them down to Jerusalem and the final feast.

The one week of His life which everybody knows is the last week. Hence we pass over it in this book. It began with the triumphant shouts of "Hosanna"; it ended with the bloodthirsty cries of "Crucify." Between the first morning of triumph and the last hours of mortal agony it witnessed His finest verbal victories over His opponents. Never were His nerves more steady, His courage higher, His mind more keen. Deliberately He piled up the mountain of hatred, knowing that it would crush Him, but determined that there should be no doubt through the ages as to *what* He had stood for and *why* He had to die. Every man who loves courageous manhood ought to read these final chapters at least once a year. Any attempt to abridge or paraphrase them would result in failure or worse. We pass over them in reverent silence, stopping only for a glimpse of the three most wonderful scenes.

First, the final supper on that cool, quiet Thursday night. He knew that He would never meet with the disciples around the table again. All the memories of the three great years must have crowded into His mind as the meal progressed. How often they had sat together under a tree beside the lake, sharing the fish that their own nets had caught. How they had enjoyed that first meal at Cana when He turned the water into wine! What a glorious afternoon it was when He fed five thousand, and the shouts of gladness echoed back and forth among the hills! And this was the end. His relatives had turned their backs on Him; His home town had scorned His advances; His best friend had died doubting; the people had turned away, and His enemies were about to triumph—is there any other leader who would have stood forth unbroken by such blows? What was *His* attitude? One of complaint? Of faultfinding? Of weak railing at His own misfortunes or the willful wickedness of men? See, He rises in His place. He speaks, this proud young man who had refused to be a king and now is to die with common thieves. And *these* are His words:

Let not your heart be troubled...(John 14:1)
I have overcome the world. (John 16:33)

There is nothing in history so majestic! Already one of His disciples had slipped away to betray Him. That very night the soldiers would take Him, bind Him, throw Him into prison. The priests and Pharisees whom He had taunted would have their turn to taunt Him now. He would be harried through the streets like a hunted thing, the butt of every corner loafer's jest. All this He anticipated, and with

153

the vision of it fresh before His mind, He lifted His head and looked beyond, into the far distant ages. "Be of good cheer," He said to them, in tones whose splendor thrills us even now. "I have overcome the world!"

They went out into the Garden where so many of their happy hours had been spent. The very air was fragrant with their most sacred confidences. Under this tree they had gathered for worship, while the setting sun gilded the towers of the city; in the waters of that brook they had found refreshment; to left and right of them the very stones cried out in heartrending reminder of the days that were gone. Even at that hour it was not too late for Him to save His life. Suppose He had said to Himself: "I have delivered my message faithfully, and it is no use. Judas has gone already to bring the soldiers; they will be here in half an hour. Why should I stay and die? It is only eighteen miles to Jericho, in bright moonlight and downhill all the way. Our friend Zacchaeus will be glad to see us. We can reach his house by daylight, rest tomorrow, cross the Jordan and do useful work the rest of our lives. The disciples can fish; I can open a carpenter shop, and teach in a quiet way. I have done everything that could be expected of me. Why not?"

It was all perfectly possible. The rulers in Jerusalem would have been glad to be rid of Him on such terms. He might so easily have continued on down the hill to peace and a comfortable old age—and oblivion. It was the last great temptation and decisively He dismissed it. He walked a little ahead in silence, followed by the eleven—for Judas was with them no longer. When they came to a quiet place, Jesus left them while He went away for His last hour of high communion with His Father, God.

His spirit was torn with agony. He was young, thirty-three. He did not want to die. He cried out to God that the cup might pass from His lips, that He might have time to sweep away the charges of blasphemy and evil which His enemies had heaped on Him, time to build up the fragile stuff of His little band on whom the whole future of His message must depend. So He prayed in agony, and in a little while returned to find them sleeping. Even so short a vigil had proved too much for their feebleness. He tried to rouse Peter with a word of gentle rebuke and warning, but Peter's heavy lids would not stay open and his ears were stopped with drowsiness.

Again He withdrew. The high tide of His revolt had subsided. The courage which had never deserted Him throughout the three years was clearing His soul, steadying His nerves. "If it be not thy will that this cup pass from me," He prayed, "then, Father, thy will be done."

He went back and found them still in deep sleep. He left them so and for the third time went a little way off. Now, with the calm peace of the conqueror without arms or armor, He could make ready for the end. Now it was full victory after battle.

On His rejoining them this time, He startled them all wide awake with the ringing word that the crucial hour

155

was at hand. They had not long to wait. The soldiers were already at the entrance of the garden. From His vantage point on the side of the hill He could mark the progress of their torches across the brook and up the path. The clang of their weapons rang through the trees; rough exclamations troubled the quiet evening air like profanity in a temple.

He waited until the armed men stumbled into His presence and then rose and stood before them.

"Whom seek ye?" He demanded.

Startled, awed, they could only mumble His name. "Jesus of Nazareth."

"I am He." The answer compounded of pride, humility, dedication.

They had expected angry denunciation, perhaps resistance—these they understood and could cope with. But such calm, such dignity, went beyond the boundaries of their experience. Involuntarily they gave way and, rough veterans that they were, some of them "fell to the ground." It was a tribute, silent but magnificent.

"I told you," He repeated calmly, "that I am He." And then His thoughts turned at once to those who had shared His triumphs and His sacrifices through the years: "If therefore ye seek me let these others go their way." But He had no need to think of the disciples' safety. Already they had made their swift escape—the last of the deserters—

    —first His home town

    —then His best friend

    —then His relatives

—then the crowd
—finally the eleven.

All who had stood at His side had gone and left Him to face His fate alone.

On a barren hill beyond the city walls they nailed His perfect body to the cross. Two robbers were crucified with Him. It was over. The rabble had sickened quickly of its revenge and scattered; His friends were hiding; the soldiers were busy casting lots for His garments. There was nothing left of the external influences which fire men's imaginations or grip their loyalty. Surely the victory of His enemies was complete; He could do no miracle there, hanging on a cross.

And yet—

"Jesus." It was the voice of one of the robbers. "Jesus," he says painfully, "remember me, *when thou comest into thy kingdom!*"

Read that, my friends, and bow your heads. You who have let yourself picture Him as weak, as a man of sorrows, uninspiring, glad to die. There have been many leaders who could call forth enthusiasm when their fortunes ran high. But He, when His enemies had done their worst, so bore Himself that a crucified felon looked into His dying eyes and saluted Him as king.

Editor's Note

This book, *The Man Nobody Knows* was originally published in 1925. The book was intended to bring the people of the early twentieth century back into the churches and reestablish a sense of religious commitment. The book topped the nonfiction best-seller lists and sold more than 750,000 copies in less than two years. Its appeal still endures even into the 21st century.

The author, Bruce Barton (1886-1967) was one of the founding members of the advertising agency Batten, Barton, Durstine and Osborne, known today as BBDO Worldwide. Among many famous advertising campaigns, Barton created the character of "Betty Crocker." Barton was elected to the U.S. House of Representatives in 1936, and for two terms he represented Manhattan's affluent "silk-stocking" district. Barton lost his bid for a Senate seat in 1940, and he returned to BBDO as the chairman until his retirement in 1961.

The style and language used in this book represents the voice of America in the 1920's. We have not changed Barton's words—to do so would dilute his message and alter his meaning.